SAS Programming and Data Visualization Techniques

A Power User's Guide

Philip R. Holland

Apress®

SAS Programming and Data Visualization Techniques: A Power User's Guide

ISBN-13 (pbk): 978-1-4842-0569-3

ISBN-13 (electronic): 978-1-4842-0568-6

Managing Director: Welmoed Spahr
Acquisitions Editor: Susan McDermott
Developmental Editor: Douglas Pundick
Technical Reviewer: Preeti Pandhu
Editorial Board: Steve Anglin, Mark Beckner, Gary Cornell, Louise Corrigan, James DeWolf, Jonathan Gennick, Robert Hutchinson, Celestin Suresh John, Michelle Lowman, James Markham, Susan McDermott, Matthew Moodie, Jeffrey Pepper, Douglas Pundick, Ben Renow-Clarke, Gwenan Spearing, Matt Wade, Steve Weiss
Coordinating Editor: Rita Fernando
Copy Editor: Tiffany Taylor
Compositor: SPi Global
Indexer: SPi Global

Distributed to the book trade worldwide by Springer Science+Business Media New York, 233 Spring Street, 6th Floor, New York, NY 10013. Phone 1-800-SPRINGER, fax (201) 348-4505, e-mail orders-ny@springer-sbm.com, or visit www.springeronline.com. Apress Media, LLC is a California LLC and the sole member (owner) is Springer Science + Business Media Finance Inc (SSBM Finance Inc). SSBM Finance Inc is a Delaware corporation.

For information on translations, please e-mail rights@apress.com, or visit www.apress.com.

Apress and friends of ED books may be purchased in bulk for academic, corporate, or promotional use. eBook versions and licenses are also available for most titles. For more information, reference our Special Bulk Sales–eBook Licensing web page at www.apress.com/bulk-sales.

Any source code or other supplementary materials referenced by the author in this text is available to readers at www.apress.com. For detailed information about how to locate your book's source code, go to www.apress.com/source-code/.

To my wife, Angela, for her tolerance and encouragement.

Contents at a Glance

Contents

About the Author

Philip R. Holland has over 30 years of experience of working with SAS software. Having started in 1981 as an MVS Systems Programmer for the University of London Computer Centre (ULCC), he moved on to Prudential Assurance, where, as an MVS Systems Programmer and Performance Analyst, he was the company's SAS technical support representative. His third and final permanent SAS position as a Capacity Planner for Centrefile ended in 1992, when he formed his own consultancy company, Holland Numerics Ltd. Since then, he has provided SAS technical consultancy and training on all major platforms that support SAS software in the financial, retail, and pharmaceutical sectors in the UK, the USA, Belgium, Holland, and Germany.

Philip is the author of numerous articles and conference papers relating to SAS and is an enthusiastic software developer, using not only SAS but also Perl, Java, JavaScript, and Visual Basic. This is his fourth SAS-related book, and his latest project has been to develop SAS-related e-book apps for Android devices and Chrome/Chromium browsers.

About the Technical Reviewer

Preeti Pandhu has a Master of Science degree in applied (industrial) statistics from the University of Pune. She is SAS certified as a base and advanced programmer for SAS 9 as well as a predictive modeler using SAS Enterprise Miner 7.

Preeti has more than 16 years of experience in analytics and training. She started her career as a lecturer in statistics and began her journey into the corporate world with IDeaS (now a SAS company), where she managed a team of business analysts in the optimization and forecasting domain. She joined SAS as a corporate trainer before stepping back into the analytics domain to contribute to a solution-testing team and research/consulting team. She was with SAS for 9 years.

Preeti is currently passionately building her analytics training firm, DataScienceLab (`www.datasciencelab.in`).

Acknowledgments

My thanks to the PhUSE Conference and SAS Global Forum committee members, for giving me the chance to present my ODS Graphics ideas at PhUSE Conferences and the SAS Global Forum.

Introduction

When selecting a technical book for myself, I tend to choose one that includes lots of examples and sample code snippets that I can use and adapt for my own development projects. I wanted to write a book that I could use for reference myself, so I have tried to make sure there are code snippets wherever possible.

As a former Performance Analyst, I still look at any programs I write to see if I can make them smaller, quicker, and/or easier to maintain. Resources may appear to be limitless, but there will inevitably come a day when a program needs more WORK disk space, more memory, more processing power, faster disk access, and so on. Part I of this book is intended to help you look at your existing programs and move that day when you run out of resources a little further into the future, thus saving money on resources and maintenance. I have spent the majority of my time as an independent consultant assisting my clients to make better use of their existing components by demonstrating new features, improving their coding efficiency, and helping them to develop applications that are easier to maintain. I want this part of my book to continue this work.

Have you ever read about a new feature in the software you already use or are thinking about using, and wondered whether it can be used in your day-to-day activities? I do this all the time, which is why the chapters in Part II focus on how to use a range of different software applications with SAS software. Although the capabilities of SAS software are constantly growing, there is always some type of functionality that SAS cannot do but that exists in another software application. Interfacing SAS and this external application can bridge the gap to achieve what you are trying to do.

I have spent the vast majority of my SAS programming career drawing graphs—first on pen plotters and, more recently, for web pages and books. SAS/GRAPH is now a vast and complicated SAS component, requiring delicate configuration that changes from platform to platform and even from graph to graph. It was a joy to find a way to draw clear graphs using Base SAS with ODS Graphics that is consistent, reusable, and, most important, simple to learn. I hope that by the end of Part III, you agree with me.

■ ■ ■

## PART I

Programming Efficiency Techniques

Overview

Throughout my career, I have worked in industries where programming performance was central to my job. This part of the book examines various aspects of programming performance:

- Chapter 1, "The Basics of Efficient SAS Coding," looks at performance in terms of the difference between the speed of program processing and program maintenance, and how to program to make maintenance easier.

- Chapter 2, "How to Use Lookup Tables Effectively," examines different techniques for merging large data sets with one or more smaller data sets, and how the performance of each technique changes with increasing data volumes.

- Chapter 3, "Case: SAS Skills in Epidemiology," explains how SAS programmers working in epidemiology use different programming techniques than those working on clinical trials, due to the greater volumes of data used in epidemiology.

CHAPTER 1

■ ■ ■

The Basics of Efficient SAS Coding

Coding efficiency is generally measured in CPU time, disk space, or memory usage. This is perfectly reasonable for SAS code that will be submitted many more times than it will be updated. However, there are coding environments where SAS programs are written for single production runs and then adapted and updated for different production runs—for example, in clinical development. In these cases, a measurement of maintenance time may be more important.

SAS programs like those used in clinical trials are unlikely to be used to process large amounts of data, but they are very likely to be updated and adapted for use in a series of trials requiring similar processing. Saving 50% of the CPU time when the program runs for only 5 minutes will not have a significant impact on coding efficiency. But if a program is difficult to maintain, days or even weeks could be added to the time needed to prepare the program for a new trial.

This chapter discusses the choices you need to make when coding efficiently in different types of SAS programs. The various situations are illustrated with coding examples.

Is the SAS Programming World "Back to Front"?

I first used PROC SQL in financial projects; many of the SAS programmers had backgrounds in database management, and SQL was routinely used. In retrospect, this was not efficient programming, because joining large SAS data sets using PROC SQL, particularly on mainframes, does not usually improve processing performance.

When I started my first clinical-trials contract, no one used PROC SQL, even though data volumes were small and SQL is much easier to read and maintain than DATA steps and PROC SORT. DATA steps and PROC SORT together are much better for working with large data volumes, whereas PROC SQL is usually better for small data volumes.

The following examples reflect my personal views on coding efficiency. In some cases, the choice of an appropriate coding approach depends on the programming experience within the SAS programming team—particularly their knowledge of SQL programming.

Speed and Low Maintenance

`IF...THEN...ELSE` and `SELECT...WHEN` constructs are examples of code that can be written to improve both speed and maintenance time. In a simple case of an input data set containing three possible values A–C for a variable, the assignment of a new variable based on the value can be written a number of ways. All three examples generate exactly the same output data set:

1. The following code is not efficient, because every `IF` condition is applied to every record. However, for small input data sets, you may not notice the inherent inefficiency:

```
DATA new;
  SET old;
  IF oldvar = 'A' THEN newvar = 1;
  IF oldvar = 'B' THEN newvar = 2;
  IF oldvar = 'C' THEN newvar = 3;
RUN;
```

2. The following code is more efficient, because `IF` conditions are applied only up to the condition that matches. However, for small input data sets, you may not notice the increased speed. You can achieve further improvements in speed by ordering the `IF` conditions so that the most commonly used is placed at the top, but this may not be worthwhile unless the data is already well-known and the most common value is very common:

```
DATA new;
  SET old;
  IF oldvar = 'A' THEN newvar = 1;
  ELSE IF oldvar = 'B' THEN newvar = 2;
  ELSE IF oldvar = 'C' THEN newvar = 3;
RUN;
```

3. The following code is comparable in efficiency to the code in example 2 in that `WHEN` conditions are applied only up to the condition that matches. For small input data sets, you may not notice the increased speed. Again, you can achieve further improvements in speed by ordering the `WHEN` conditions so that the most commonly used is placed at the top. In my opinion, this construct is easier to maintain, because all the lines have the same layout; thus you can insert or delete lines with a reduced risk of introducing syntax errors. The mandatory `OTHERWISE` clause also provides an obvious place to include a default value if none of the previous conditions have been fulfilled:

```
DATA new;
  SET old;
  SELECT (oldvar);
    WHEN ('A') newvar = 1;
    WHEN ('B') newvar = 2;
    WHEN ('C') newvar = 3;
    OTHERWISE;
  END;
RUN;
```

Extending conditional clauses to 10 or more conditions requires great care to avoid inefficient processing, especially if the input data set is large. You can also avoid inefficient maintenance, particularly if the conditional code is enclosed in a DO...END construct, if you lay out the code with indents indicating the relative positions of each section of conditional code.

Speed or Low Maintenance: Part 1

Rewriting a data-step merge with a PROC SQL join can help reduce maintenance time but may reduce processing speed. The following sample code merges three data sets using two variables and then reorders the resulting data set by another variable:

1. This is a combination of PROC SORT and DATA steps. The code is efficient as far as processing is concerned, but it is quite long and involved, because you have to sort the individual data sets prior to merging them:

```
PROC SORT DATA = a OUT = a1;
  BY cat_b;
RUN;

PROC SORT DATA = b OUT = b1;
  BY cat_b;
RUN;

DATA a1_b1;
  MERGE a1 (IN = a) b1 (IN = b);
  BY cat_b;
  IF a AND b;
RUN;

PROC SORT DATA = a1_b1 OUT = a1_b11;
  BY cat_c;
RUN;

PROC SORT DATA = c OUT = c1;
  BY cat_c;
RUN;

DATA a1_b1_c1;
  MERGE a1_b11 (IN = ab) c1 (IN = c);
  BY cat_c;
  IF ab AND c;
RUN;

PROC SORT DATA = a1_b1_c1;
  BY cat_a cat_b cat_c;
RUN;
```

2. This is a single PROC SQL step that does everything in the one step, including the final sort. When input data sets are small to moderate in size, there is little difference in the CPU time used by this and the previous code, but very large input data sets can result in slower processing when using PROC SQL. Another obvious disadvantage is that, when combining two or more data sets with overlapping variables, you must list all the variables to be included in the output data sets. However, assuming the SAS programming team has some experience with SQL programming, this program should be easier to maintain:

```
PROC SQL;
  CREATE TABLE a_b_c AS
    SELECT a.cat_a
          ,b.cat_b
          ,c.cat_c
          ,a.num_a1
          ,a.num_a2
          ,b.num_b1
          ,b.num_b2
          ,c.num_c1
          ,c.num_c2
    FROM    a
          ,b
          ,c
    WHERE   a.cat_b = b.cat_b
      AND   a.cat_c = c.cat_c
    ORDER BY
            a.cat_a
          ,b.cat_b
          ,c.cat_c
    ;
QUIT;
```

Speed or Low Maintenance: Part 2

Coding simple merges is fairly straightforward using DATA or PROC SQL steps, but PROC SQL may be the number-one choice when you are joining tables based on a range of values, rather than a one-to-one match. In this example, the code is being used to calculate the largest difference between records within 28 days of each other:

1. This is a combination of PROC SORT, PROC TRANSPOSE, and DATA steps, which can be efficient as far as processing is concerned but is quite long and involved because you have to use arrays to categorize all the individual pairs of records:

```
PROC SORT DATA = old OUT = temp;
  BY cat;
RUN;

DATA temp;
  SET temp;
  BY cat;
  RETAIN order;
```

```
      IF FIRST.cat THEN order = 1;
      ELSE order + 1;
   RUN;

   PROC TRANSPOSE DATA = temp OUT = num PREFIX = num;
     BY cat;
     VAR num;
     ID order;
   RUN;

   PROC TRANSPOSE DATA = temp OUT = val PREFIX = val;
     BY cat;
     VAR val;
     ID order;
   RUN;

   DATA all (DROP = _:);
     MERGE num val;
     BY cat;
   RUN;

   DATA new (KEEP = cat maxval);
     SET all;
     BY cat;
     ARRAY num num:;
     ARRAY val val:;
     ARRAY test test1-test50;
     maxval = .;
     reset = 1;
     DO i = 1 TO DIM(num);
       DO j = i+1 TO DIM(num);
         IF num(j) - num(i) LE 28
            AND ROUND(val(j) - val(i), .0001) GT maxval
           THEN maxval = ROUND(val(j) - val(i), .0001);
       END;
     END;
     IF LAST.cat THEN OUTPUT;
   RUN;
```

2. This uses two PROC SQL steps: one to join the input data set with itself to generate all possible combinations of 1- to 28-day gaps, and a second PROC SQL step to find the largest value difference. Again, when the input data sets are small to moderate in size, there is little difference in CPU time between this and the previous code; but very large input data sets can result in slower processing when using PROC SQL. But assuming the SAS programming team has some experience with SQL programming, this program should be much easier to maintain:

```
PROC SQL;
  CREATE TABLE temp AS
    SELECT b1.cat
          ,b1.num
          ,MAX(b2.val - b1.val) AS maxval
```

```
          FROM    old b1
          LEFT JOIN
                  old b2
          ON      b1.cat = b2.cat
             AND  (b2.num - b1.num) BETWEEN 1 AND 28
          GROUP BY
                  b1.cat
                 ,b1.num
       ;
    QUIT;

    PROC SQL;
      CREATE TABLE new AS
        SELECT cat
              ,MAX(maxval) AS maxval
        FROM   temp
        GROUP BY
                cat
       ;
    QUIT;
```

Personal Preferences

Every SAS programming team has its own "standard" reporting procedure, usually PROC REPORT or PROC TABULATE. In terms of processing time, there is little difference between them. But, strangely, combining PROC SUMMARY and PROC PRINT can create very acceptable tables in less processing time. As far as maintenance time is concerned, the choice depends on what you are used to:

1. PROC REPORT is compact and easy to maintain. The order of the report columns is determined by the COLUMN statement:

    ```
    PROC REPORT DATA = old NOWD;
      TITLE "Report";
      COLUMN cat_a cat_b = n_b cat_b = pct_b num val;
      DEFINE cat_a / GROUP 'Category';
      DEFINE n_b / SUM FORMAT = 8. 'N b';
      DEFINE pct_b / MEAN FORMAT = PERCENT8. 'Pct b';
      DEFINE num / MEAN FORMAT = 8.1 'Mean num';
      DEFINE val / MEDIAN FORMAT = 8.1 'Median val';
    RUN;
    ```

2. PROC TABULATE has a more complex syntax but is easier to use when you need to include multiple statistics for a single variable. All you have to remember is that the syntax follows the simple rule [[[Page,] Row,] Column]:

    ```
    PROC TABULATE DATA = old;
      TITLE "Tabulate";
      CLASS cat_a;
      VAR cat_b num val;
      TABLE cat_a = 'Category'
              ,(cat_b = ' ' * (SUM = 'N b' * F = 8.
                               MEAN = 'Pct b' * F = PERCENT8.)
    ```

```
              num = ' ' * MEAN = 'Mean num' * F = 8.1
              val = ' ' * MEDIAN = 'Median val' * F = 8.1
            )
          ;
    RUN;
```

3. PROC PRINT is often ignored, but with PROC SUMMARY it makes a useful alternative, with simple syntax and fast processing:

```
PROC SUMMARY DATA = old NWAY;
  CLASS cat_a;
  VAR cat_b num val;
  OUTPUT OUT = temp SUM(cat_b) = n_b
                    MEAN(cat_b num) = pct_b num
                    MEDIAN(val)=
                    ;
RUN;

PROC PRINT DATA = temp LABEL;
  TITLE "SUMMARY + PRINT";
  VAR cat_a n_b pct_b num val;
  LABEL cat_a = 'Category'
        n_b = 'N b'
        pct_b = 'Pct b'
        num = 'Mean num'
        val = 'Median val'
        ;
  FORMAT n_b 8.
         pct_b PERCENT8.
         num val 8.1
         ;
RUN;
```

Reducing Maintenance: Part 1

In the following examples, the PROC SQL code is exactly the same. But, in my opinion, coding layout 3 is easier to maintain, because all the lines have the same layout—you can insert or delete lines with a reduced risk of introducing syntax errors:

1. This is a *prose* layout, which is quick to write but can be a nightmare to maintain:

```
PROC SQL;
  CREATE TABLE new AS SELECT a.col1, b.col2, a.col3 FROM a, b
  WHERE a.col1 = b.col1 AND a.col2 = b.col2;
QUIT;
```

2. This *split* layout is easier to read, but inserting and deleting lines of code can introduce syntax errors:

```
PROC SQL;
  CREATE TABLE new AS
    SELECT a.col1,
           b.col2,
```

```
                a.col3
    FROM a,
         b
    WHERE a.col1 = b.col1 AND
          a.col2 = b.col2;
QUIT;
```

3. This is a *comma-first* layout, which is easier to read and which lets you insert
    and delete lines of code safely. Note that bolded lines are always written with
    commas and operators at the beginning of each line so that they can be safely
    duplicated or deleted:

```
PROC SQL;
  CREATE TABLE new AS
    SELECT a.col1
           ,b.col2
           ,a.col3
    FROM   a
           ,b
    WHERE  a.col1 = b.col1
      AND  a.col2 = b.col2
  ;
QUIT;
```

Reducing Maintenance: Part 2

How else can you reduce the effort required to maintain code in the future? The following examples have
exactly the same functionality:

1. This is unsubstituted SQL:

```
PROC SQL;
 CREATE TABLE temp AS
   SELECT b1.cat
          ,b1.num
          ,MAX(b2.val-b1.val) AS maxval
   FROM   old b1
   LEFT JOIN
          old b2
   ON     b1.cat = b2.cat
     AND  (b2.num-b1.num) BETWEEN 1 AND 28
   GROUP BY
          b1.cat
          ,b1.num;
QUIT;
```

2. This is parameterized SQL, which requires less effort to maintain:

```
%LET d = 28;
%LET c = cat;
%LET n = num;
%LET v = val;
```

```
PROC SQL;
 CREATE TABLE temp AS
  SELECT b1.&c.
         ,b1.&n.
         ,MAX(b2.&v.-b1.&v.) AS maxval
  FROM    old b1
  LEFT JOIN
          old b2
  ON      b1.&c. = b2.&c.
    AND   (b2.&n.-b1.&n.) BETWEEN 1 AND &d.
  GROUP BY
          b1.&c.
         ,b1.&n.;
QUIT;
```

Conclusions

The following conclusions are based on my own experience:

- Any section of code used to create a single variable that cannot be printed on a single side of A4 or Letter paper is too complex.

- If you are processing a small amount of data, then saving 50% of the processing time by spending 50% more development time is not efficient coding.

- High speed and low maintenance time mean efficient coding.

- Low speed and high maintenance time mean inefficient coding.

- The efficiency of coding with high speed and high maintenance time, or low speed and low maintenance time, depends on how often the program is submitted.

References

- SAS Training Course: SAS Programming 3: Advanced Techniques and Efficiencies, https://support.sas.com/edu/schedules.html?id=1917.

CHAPTER 2

■ ■ ■

How to Use Lookup Tables Effectively

There are many different ways to combine small lookup tables with larger SAS data sets. This chapter shows how to use the most appropriate and efficient method, depending on the circumstances.

No matter what type of programming you do in any SAS programming environment, there will eventually be a need to combine your data with a lookup table. This lookup table may be a code list for adverse events, a list of names for visits, or just one of your own summary data sets containing totals that you will be using to calculate percentages, and you may have your favorite way to incorporate it. This chapter describes, and discusses the reasons for, using six different simple ways to merge data sets with lookup tables. After reading this chapter, when you take over the maintenance of a new program, you will be ready for anything!

Sample Data Sets

All six techniques described in this chapter use the same four SAS data sets to create the same output data set. These data sets are as follows:

- MAIN includes multiple copies of SASHELP.CARS (428 observations and 15 variables) saved in a single WORK data set to increase the size of this data set:

```
%LET mult = 1;   /* 10, 100, 1000, 2000, 5000 */

DATA main;
    SET sashelp.cars;
    DO i = 1 TO &mult.;
        OUTPUT;
    END;
RUN;
```

- LOOKUP_ORIGIN (3 observations and 3 variables) is shown in Figure 2-1:

```
PROC SQL;
    CREATE TABLE lookup_origin AS

        SELECT origin  /* key */
                ,COUNT(DISTINCT make) AS make_n
                ,COUNT(DISTINCT type) AS type_n
```

```
            FROM    sashelp.cars
            GROUP BY
                    origin
            ORDER BY
                    origin
        ;
    QUIT;
```

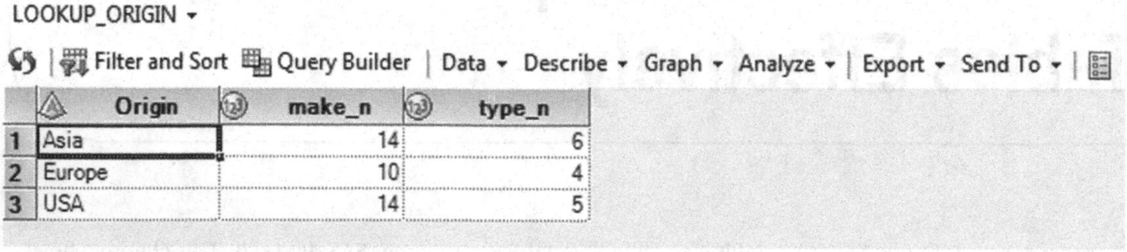

LOOKUP_ORIGIN ▾

🔄 | 🔽 Filter and Sort 📊 Query Builder | Data ▾ Describe ▾ Graph ▾ Analyze ▾ | Export ▾ Send To ▾ | 🗒

	Origin	make_n	type_n
1	Asia	14	6
2	Europe	10	4
3	USA	14	5

Figure 2-1. *LOOKUP_ORIGIN data set*

- LOOKUP_TYPE (15 observations and 6 variables) is shown in Figure 2-2:

```
PROC SQL;
    CREATE TABLE lookup_type AS
        SELECT origin, type  /* keys */
                ,COUNT(DISTINCT model) AS type_model_n
                ,COUNT(DISTINCT make) AS type_make_n
                ,MEAN(msrp) AS type_msrp_mean
                ,MAX(horsepower) AS type_horsepower_max
        FROM    sashelp.cars
        GROUP BY
                origin, type
        ORDER BY
                origin, type
    ;
    QUIT;
```

LOOKUP_TYPE ▾

⟳ | 🔳 Filter and Sort 🔳 Query Builder | Data ▾ Describe ▾ Graph ▾ Analyze ▾ | Export ▾ Send To ▾ | 🔳

	Origin	Type	type_model_n	type_make_n	type_msrp_mean	type_horsepower_max
1	Asia	Hybrid	3	2	19920	110
2	Asia	SUV	25	11	29569	325
3	Asia	Sedan	93	13	22763.968085	340
4	Asia	Sports	17	9	32510.647059	300
5	Asia	Truck	8	4	20383.625	305
6	Asia	Wagon	11	9	23143.727273	315
7	Europe	SUV	10	6	48346	340
8	Europe	Sedan	76	8	42992.051282	493
9	Europe	Sports	23	5	71998.695652	493
10	Europe	Wagon	12	6	37851.25	340
11	USA	SUV	25	12	34589.2	325
12	USA	Sedan	90	12	25638.833333	302
13	USA	Sports	9	6	45257.222222	500
14	USA	Truck	16	5	27220.25	345
15	USA	Wagon	7	6	22345.714286	250

Figure 2-2. *LOOKUP_TYPE data set*

- LOOKUP_MAKE (38 observations and 6 variables) is partially shown in Figure 2-3:

```
PROC SQL;
    CREATE TABLE lookup_make AS
        SELECT origin, make  /* keys */
                ,COUNT(DISTINCT model) AS make_model_n
                ,COUNT(DISTINCT type) AS make_type_n
                ,MEAN(msrp) AS make_msrp_mean
                ,MAX(horsepower) AS make_horsepower_max
        FROM    sashelp.cars
        GROUP BY
                origin, make
        ORDER BY
                origin, make
    ;
QUIT;
```

LOOKUP_MAKE ▾

🕙 | 🏯 Filter and Sort 🏭 Query Builder | Data ▾ Describe ▾ Graph ▾ Analyze ▾ | Export ▾ Send To ▾ | 🖿

	Origin		Make	make_model_n	make_type_n	make_msrp_mean	make_horsepower_max
1	Asia		Acura	7	3	42938.571429	290
2	Asia		Honda	17	4	21434.705882	240
3	Asia		Hyundai	12	3	17476.5	194
4	Asia		Infiniti	7	2	36070	340
5	Asia		Isuzu	2	1	26149	275
6	Asia		Kia	11	3	15875.909091	195
7	Asia		Lexus	11	4	44215.454545	300
8	Asia		Mazda	11	4	21770.727273	238
9	Asia		Mitsubishi	13	4	23423.615385	271
10	Asia		Nissan	17	5	24730.941176	305
11	Asia		Scion	2	2	13565	108
12	Asia		Subaru	11	4	25501.818182	300
13	Asia		Suzuki	8	3	16230.25	185
14	Asia		Toyota	28	6	22524.464286	325
15	Europe		Audi	19	3	43307.894737	450
16	Europe		BMW	20	4	43285.25	333
17	Europe		Jaguar	12	2	61580.416667	390
18	Europe		Land Rover	3	1	45831.666667	282
19	Europe		MINI	2	1	18499	163
20	Europe		Mercedes-Benz	24	4	60656.807692	493
21	Europe		Porsche	7	2	83565	477
22	Europe		Saab	7	2	37640	250
23	Europe		Volkswagen	15	3	32648.666667	420
24	Europe		Volvo	12	3	36314.166667	300
25	USA		Buick	9	2	30537.777778	275
26	USA		Cadillac	8	4	50474.375	345
27	USA		Chevrolet	27	5	26587.037037	350
28	USA		Chrysler	15	3	27252	255
29	USA		Dodge	13	4	26253.846154	500
30	USA		Ford	23	5	24015.869565	310
31	USA		GMC	8	3	29560.5	325

Figure 2-3. LOOKUP_MAKE data set

DATA Step Merge

This is probably the most commonly used technique to merge SAS data sets. The SAS environment was originally built around the DATA step, so the technique has been included in SAS training courses for a very long time. However, it is also one of the least efficient methods, because, for each join, the two data sets must be sorted the same way. In this example, even though the smaller lookup data sets would be quicker to sort, the large master data set has to resorted each time.

The output data set will include four new calculated variables:

- `make_msrp_flag`, which is set to 1 if msrp > mean msrp by make.

- `make_horsepower_pct`, which is set to the percentage of the maximum horsepower by make

- `type_msrp_flag`, which is set to 1 if msrp > mean msrp by type

- type_horsepower_pct, which is set to the percentage of the maximum horsepower by type

```
PROC SORT DATA = main OUT = datastepmerge1; BY origin make; RUN;

DATA datastepmerge2;
    MERGE datastepmerge1 lookup_origin;
    BY origin;
RUN;

DATA datastepmerge3;
    MERGE datastepmerge2 lookup_make;
    BY origin make;
    IF msrp > make_msrp_mean THEN make_msrp_flag = 1;
                             ELSE make_msrp_flag = 0;
    make_horsepower_pct = 100 * horsepower / make_horsepower_max;
RUN;

PROC SORT DATA = datastepmerge3 OUT = datastepmerge4; BY origin type; RUN;

DATA datastepmerge5;
    MERGE datastepmerge4 lookup_type;
    BY origin type;
    IF msrp > type_msrp_mean THEN type_msrp_flag = 1;
                             ELSE type_msrp_flag = 0;
    type_horsepower_pct = 100 * horsepower / type_horsepower_max;
RUN;
```

SQL Join

The strange fact about PROC SQL is that it becomes less efficient with increasing data, yet it is rarely used with clinical data, where the data volumes are low, but widely used with financial data, where the data volumes are high. The reason for this anomaly is that SQL is heavily used by database administrators, and many SAS programmers working with financial data have had database administrator training. So, rather than changing their working practices, they continue to use the programming environment where they are comfortable:

```
PROC SQL;
    CREATE TABLE sqljoin1 AS
```

Copy all the variables from the a data set (main), along with the new variables from the lookup tables (b=lookup_origin, c=lookup_make and d=lookup_type):

```
SELECT a.*
    ,b.make_n
    ,b.type_n
    ,c.make_model_n
    ,c.make_type_n
    ,c.make_msrp_mean
    ,c.make_horsepower_max
```

```
   ,d.type_model_n
   ,d.type_make_n
   ,d.type_msrp_mean
   ,d.type_horsepower_max
```

Calculate the percentages using the SQL expression syntax:

```
,(100 * a.horsepower / c.make_horsepower_max) AS make_horsepower_pct
,(100 * a.horsepower / d.type_horsepower_max) AS type_horsepower_pct
```

The CASE construct is the SQL equivalent of the DATA step IF statement:

```
   ,(CASE
     WHEN a.msrp > c.make_msrp_mean THEN 1
     ELSE 0
     END) AS make_msrp_flag

   ,(CASE
     WHEN a.msrp > d.type_msrp_mean THEN 1
     ELSE 0
     END) AS type_msrp_flag

FROM   main a
```

The lookup tables are merged with main using a LEFT JOIN:

```
   LEFT JOIN
          lookup_origin b
   ON     a.origin = b.origin
   LEFT JOIN
          lookup_make c
   ON     a.origin = c.origin AND a.make = c.make
   LEFT JOIN
          lookup_type d
   ON     a.origin = d.origin AND a.type = d.type
   ;
QUIT;
```

Generated SAS Formats

Using SAS formats is inherently more efficient than joining data sets directly, because the format data is stored in memory rather than on disk. There is a small downside—you have to convert the data sets into formats—but these data sets are relatively small, so there is a significant benefit to using SAS formats as lookup tables. Available memory is a limiting factor for the usable size of the format, but formats in excess of 50,000 entries are perfectly acceptable:

```
DATA format_origin;
    LENGTH fmtname $7 start $80 label 8 type hlo $1;
    SET lookup_origin;
    type = 'I';
```

```
        hlo = ' ';
        start = origin;
        fmtname = 'originm';
        label = make_n;
        output;
        fmtname = 'origint';
        label = type_n;
        output;
RUN;

PROC SORT DATA = format_origin NODUPKEY; BY fmtname start; RUN;

PROC FORMAT CNTLIN = format_origin; RUN;
```

Remember to rename the level1= variable to prevent a clash between TYPE and the required variable of the same name in the CNTLIN data set:

```
%MACRO generate_format(level1=, level2=);
    DATA format_&level1.;
        LENGTH fmtname $7 start $80 label 8 type hlo $1;
        SET lookup_&level1.`(RENAME = (&level1.=level1));
        type = 'I';
        hlo = ' ';
        start = CATX('|', origin, &level1.);
        fmtname = "&level1.c";
        label = &level1._model_n;
        output;
        fmtname = "&level1.x";
        label = &level1._&level2._n;
        output;
        fmtname = "&level1.p";
        label = &level1._msrp_mean;
        output;
        fmtname = "&level1.h";
        label = &level1._horsepower_max;
        output;
    RUN;

    PROC SORT DATA = format_&level1. NODUPKEY; BY fmtname start; RUN;

    PROC FORMAT CNTLIN = format_&level1.; RUN;
%MEND generate_format;

%generate_format(level1=make, level2=type);
%generate_format(level1=type, level2=make);

DATA format1;
    SET main;
    make_n = INPUT(origin, originm.);
    type_n = INPUT(origin, origint.);
    make_model_n = INPUT(CATX('|', origin, make), makec.);
```

```
   make_type_n = INPUT(CATX('|', origin, make), makex.);
   make_msrp_mean = INPUT(CATX('|', origin, make), makep.);
   IF msrp > make_msrp_mean THEN make_msrp_flag = 1;
                            ELSE make_msrp_flag = 0;
   make_horsepower_max = INPUT(CATX('|', origin, make), makeh.);
   make_horsepower_pct = 100 * horsepower / make_horsepower_max;
   type_model_n = INPUT(CATX('|', origin, type), typec.);
   type_make_n = INPUT(CATX('|', origin, type), typex.);
   type_msrp_mean = INPUT(CATX('|', origin, type), typep.);
   IF msrp > type_msrp_mean THEN type_msrp_flag = 1;
                            ELSE type_msrp_flag = 0;
   type_horsepower_max = INPUT(CATX('|', origin, type), typeh.);
   type_horsepower_pct = 100 * horsepower / type_horsepower_max;
RUN;
```

It is often helpful to see what the generated data looks like, so the data in format_origin is shown in Figure 2-4.

format_origin

Obs	fmtname	start	label	type	hlo
1	originm	Asia	14	I	
2	originm	Europe	10	I	
3	originm	USA	14	I	
4	origint	Asia	6	I	
5	origint	Europe	4	I	
6	origint	USA	5	I	

Figure 2-4. The data generated in format_origin

Generated If .. Then .. Else

To save all the sorting and memory usage, why not generate DATA step code to add the extra information from the lookup data sets? In this case, IF .. THEN .. ELSE statements are generated from the lookup data sets and stored as text records in a SAS Catalog Source entry in a WORK catalog so that they are deleted automatically at the end of the SAS session:

```
FILENAME srcif CATALOG "work.generateif";

DATA _NULL_;
   SET lookup_origin END = eof;
   FILE srcif(origin.source);
   IF _N_ = 1 THEN PUT "IF origin = '" origin +(-1) "' THEN DO;";
   ELSE PUT "ELSE IF origin = '" origin +(-1) "' THEN DO;";
```

```
        PUT "make_n = " make_n ";";
        PUT "type_n = " type_n ";";
        PUT "END;";
RUN;

%MACRO generate_if(level1=, level2=);
    DATA _NULL_;
        SET lookup_&level1. END = eof;
        FILE srcif(&level1..source);
        IF _N_ = 1 THEN PUT "IF origin = '" origin +(-1) "' AND &level1. = '"
                            &level1. +(-1) "' THEN DO;";
        ELSE PUT "ELSE IF origin = '" origin +(-1) "' AND &level1. = '"
                 &level1. +(-1) "' THEN DO;";
        PUT "&level1._model_n = " &level1._model_n ";";
        PUT "&level1._&level2._n = " &level1._&level2._n ";";
        PUT "&level1._msrp_mean = " &level1._msrp_mean ";";
        PUT "IF msrp > &level1._msrp_mean THEN &level1._msrp_flag = 1;";
        PUT "                             ELSE &level1._msrp_flag = 0;";
        PUT "&level1._horsepower_max = " &level1._horsepower_max ";";
        PUT "&level1._horsepower_pct = 100 * horsepower / &level1._horsepower_max;";
        PUT "END;";
    RUN;
%MEND generate_if;

%generate_if(level1=make, level2=type);
%generate_if(level1=type, level2=make);

DATA generateif1;
    SET main;
    %INCLUDE srcif(origin.source);
    %INCLUDE srcif(make.source);
    %INCLUDE srcif(type.source);
RUN;
```

An extract from the SAS code generated in srcif(type.source) is shown in Figure 2-5.

```
IF origin = 'Asia' AND type = 'Hybrid' THEN DO;
type_model_n = 3 ;
type_make_n = 2 ;
type_msrp_mean = 19920 ;
IF msrp > type_msrp_mean THEN type_msrp_flag = 1;
                         ELSE type_msrp_flag = 0;
type_horsepower_max = 110 ;
type_horsepower_pct = 100 * horsepower / type_horsepower_max;
END;
ELSE IF origin = 'Asia' AND type = 'SUV' THEN DO;
type_model_n = 25 ;
type_make_n = 11 ;
type_msrp_mean = 29569 ;
IF msrp > type_msrp_mean THEN type_msrp_flag = 1;
                         ELSE type_msrp_flag = 0;
type_horsepower_max = 325 ;
type_horsepower_pct = 100 * horsepower / type_horsepower_max;
END;
ELSE IF origin = 'Asia' AND type = 'Sedan' THEN DO;
type_model_n = 93 ;
type_make_n = 13 ;
type_msrp_mean = 22763.968085 ;
IF msrp > type_msrp_mean THEN type_msrp_flag = 1;
                         ELSE type_msrp_flag = 0;
type_horsepower_max = 340 ;
type_horsepower_pct = 100 * horsepower / type_horsepower_max;
END;
```

Figure 2-5. *An extract from the SAS code generated in* srcif(type.source)

Generated Select .. When .. Otherwise

In this case, SELECT .. WHEN .. OTHERWISE statements are generated from the lookup data sets and stored as text records in a SAS Catalog Source entry in a WORK catalog so that they are deleted automatically at the end of the SAS session. The advantage of these statements over IF .. THEN .. ELSE is that the OTHERWISE statement forces an action if none of the previous tests are satisfied, and thus it can be used to highlight any omissions:

```
FILENAME srcsel CATALOG "work.generateselect";

DATA _NULL_;
    SET lookup_origin END = eof;
    FILE srcsel(origin.source);
    IF _N_ = 1 THEN PUT "SELECT;";
    PUT "WHEN (origin = '" origin +(-1) "') DO;";
    PUT "make_n = " make_n ";";
    PUT "type_n = " type_n ";";
```

```
        PUT "END;";
        IF eof THEN DO;
            PUT "OTHERWISE;";
            PUT "END;";
        END;
RUN;

%MACRO generate_select(level1=, level2=);
    DATA _NULL_;
        SET lookup_&level1. END = eof;
        FILE srcsel(&level1..source);
        IF _N_ = 1 THEN PUT "SELECT;";
        PUT "WHEN (origin = '" origin +(-1) "' AND &level1. = '" &level1. +(-1) "') DO;";
        PUT "&level1._model_n = " &level1._model_n ";";
        PUT "&level1._&level2._n = " &level1._&level2._n ";";
        PUT "&level1._msrp_mean = " &level1._msrp_mean ";";
        PUT "IF msrp > &level1._msrp_mean THEN &level1._msrp_flag = 1;";
        PUT "                              ELSE &level1._msrp_flag = 0;";
        PUT "&level1._horsepower_max = " &level1._horsepower_max ";";
        PUT "&level1._horsepower_pct = 100 * horsepower / &level1._horsepower_max;";
        PUT "END;";
        IF eof THEN DO;
            PUT "OTHERWISE;";
            PUT "END;";
        END;
    RUN;
%MEND generate_select;

%generate_select(level1=make, level2=type);
%generate_select(level1=type, level2=make);

DATA generateselect1;
    SET main;
    %INCLUDE srcsel(origin.source);
    %INCLUDE srcsel(make.source);
    %INCLUDE srcsel(type.source);
RUN;
```

An extract from the SAS code generated in srcsel(make.source) is shown in Figure 2-6.

```
SELECT;
WHEN (origin = 'Asia' AND make = 'Acura') DO;
make_model_n = 7 ;
make_type_n = 3 ;
make_msrp_mean = 42938.571429 ;
IF msrp > make_msrp_mean THEN make_msrp_flag = 1;
                           ELSE make_msrp_flag = 0;
make_horsepower_max = 290 ;
make_horsepower_pct = 100 * horsepower / make_horsepower_max;
END;
WHEN (origin = 'Asia' AND make = 'Honda') DO;
make_model_n = 17 ;
make_type_n = 4 ;
make_msrp_mean = 21434.705882 ;
IF msrp > make_msrp_mean THEN make_msrp_flag = 1;
                           ELSE make_msrp_flag = 0;
make_horsepower_max = 240 ;
make_horsepower_pct = 100 * horsepower / make_horsepower_max;
END;
WHEN (origin = 'Asia' AND make = 'Hyundai') DO;
make_model_n = 12 ;
make_type_n = 3 ;
make_msrp_mean = 17476.5 ;
IF msrp > make_msrp_mean THEN make_msrp_flag = 1;
                           ELSE make_msrp_flag = 0;
make_horsepower_max = 194 ;
make_horsepower_pct = 100 * horsepower / make_horsepower_max;
END;
```

Figure 2-6. *An extract from the SAS code generated in* `srcsel(make.source)`

DATA Step Hash

Mentioning hash joins to many SAS programmers can generate fear and apprehension. In fact, this technique is not that difficult to use, although it does involve some very unfamiliar SAS syntax. Everything can be achieved in a single DATA step:

- IF 0 THEN is a trick to let the DATA step parser read the internal structure of an input data set without any data being read by that statement during execution.

- DECLARE HASH uses HASHEXP:7 to size the hash internal table, where the table is $2^7 = 128$ containers. DATASET is used to specify the lookup table.

- DEFINEKEY is used to specify the lookup variable(s).

- DEFINEDATA, in this case, specifies that all of the lookup data is used.

- DEFINEDONE completes the setup:

```
DATA hash;
    /* create origin hash */
    IF O THEN SET lookup_origin;
    DECLARE HASH lookup_origin(HASHEXP:7, DATASET:'lookup_origin');
    lookup_origin.DEFINEKEY('origin');
    lookup_origin.DEFINEDATA(ALL:'Y');
    lookup_origin.DEFINEDONE();
    /* create make hash */
    IF O THEN SET lookup_make;
    DECLARE HASH lookup_make(HASHEXP:7, DATASET:'lookup_make');
    lookup_make.DEFINEKEY('origin', 'make');
    lookup_make.DEFINEDATA(ALL:'Y');
    lookup_make.DEFINEDONE();
    /* create type hash */
    IF O THEN SET lookup_type;
    DECLARE HASH lookup_type(HASHEXP:7, DATASET:'lookup_type');
    lookup_type.DEFINEKEY('origin', 'type');
    lookup_type.DEFINEDATA(ALL:'Y');
    lookup_type.DEFINEDONE();
```

Now loop through the main data set using the FIND() function to test for matches using each hash table. This does not appear to make sense, but FIND() = 0 means a match has been found. In other words, the return code is 0:

```
DO UNTIL (eof);
    SET main END = eof;
    /* search origin hash */
    IF lookup_origin.FIND() = O THEN DO;
        /* nothing to do here */
    END;
    ELSE CALL MISSING(make_n, type_n);
    /* search make hash */
    IF lookup_make.FIND() = O THEN DO;
        IF msrp > make_msrp_mean THEN make_msrp_flag = 1;
                            ELSE make_msrp_flag = 0;
        make_horsepower_pct = 100 * horsepower / make_horsepower_max;
    END;
    ELSE CALL MISSING(make_model_n, make_type_n, make_msrp_mean, make_horsepower_max,
                    make_msrp_flag, make_horsepower_pct);
    /* search type hash */
    IF lookup_type.FIND() = O THEN DO;
        IF msrp > type_msrp_mean THEN type_msrp_flag = 1;
                            ELSE type_msrp_flag = 0;
        type_horsepower_pct = 100 * horsepower / type_horsepower_max;
    END;
    ELSE CALL MISSING(type_model_n, type_make_n, type_msrp_mean, type_horsepower_max,
                    type_msrp_flag, type_horsepower_pct);
    /* output each record */
    OUTPUT;
    END;
    STOP;
RUN;
```

25

Conclusions

Any discussion of performance of coding techniques needs to be supported by evidence. Comparing techniques using CPU time, as shown in Figure 2-7, you can see that DATA step merges and SQL joins are comparable, formats are quicker, and the DATA step statement-generating techniques are still quicker, but the DATA step hash is the quickest. Note that CPU time is not generally seen as an important measure when the SAS platform is not supporting a large number of concurrent users.

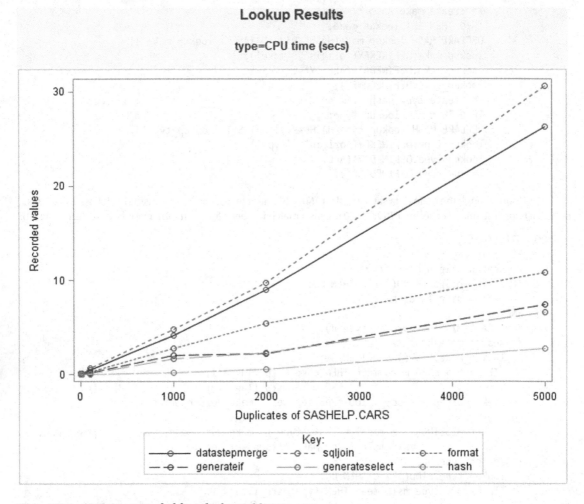

Figure 2-7. CPU time recorded from lookup table tests

Comparing techniques using elapsed time is more interesting, as you can see in Figure 2-8. All the techniques show a linear increase in elapsed time, apart from SQL join, for which elapsed time increases dramatically as the volume increases after being fairly fast at low data volumes. This is because, at low data volumes, PROC SQL carries out most of its data processing in memory. At higher data volumes, it is forced to use the WORK library to store intermediate data, because disk access is much less efficient than accessing memory. Both DATA step merge and SQL join are significantly less efficient than the other three techniques, which minimize the number of data passes.

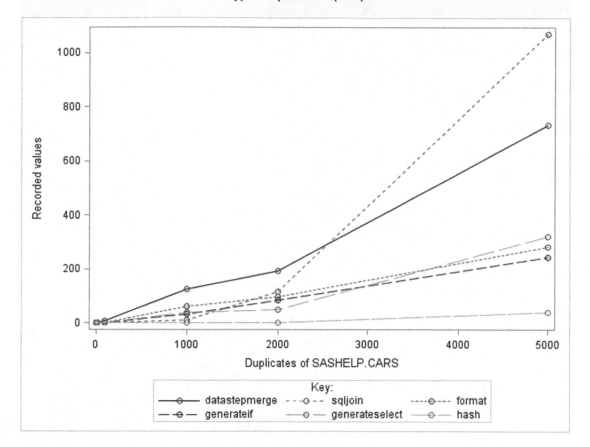

Figure 2-8. *Elapsed time recorded from lookup table tests*

Are you now considering a new technique for using lookup tables?

Reference

- SAS Training Course: SAS Programming 3: Advanced Techniques and Efficiencies, https://support.sas.com/edu/schedules.html?id=1917.

■ ■ ■

## CHAPTER 3

Case: SAS Skills in Epidemiology

In epidemiology, most data sets from SAS and other databases are big, and SAS programmers need particular skills to work with the data. This case illustrates principles that are useful for programmers dealing with large databases in all industries.

SAS programmers in epidemiology departments require very different skills than those working on clinical trials, because of the sheer size, complexity, and irregular nature of the data used. This chapter will investigate the skills required, and suggests that recruiting programmers with skills from outside the pharmaceutical sector may not be such a bad idea.

Size Really Is Important!

A major difference between epidemiology and clinical trials is the amount of data that a SAS programmer must be able to cope with. Data sets are routinely measured in gigabytes, not megabytes, and you should reduce the data volume as much as possible before performing any processing by keeping only the columns you need and by using a subset of the data set records. Even then, you should keep data sorting to a minimum, consider at every step the amount of data stored in WORK, and expect processing to take hours rather than minutes.

Working with Longitudinal Databases

SAS programmers in epidemiology use longitudinal databases in which patient details, medical events, and prescriptions are selected separately from different files and then combined as required. This is similar to the approach used with data in clinical trials, but the medical events and prescriptions in this case occur at random times. Also, because each disease and therapeutic area has different coding requirements, only a little of the SAS code is reusable; more often than not, a new program has to be written for each analysis.

If a SAS programmers who had previously worked with credit card data were to analyze this data, they would probably see that the following:

- The patients are like credit cards.

- All medical events and prescriptions are like credit card transactions.

- Disease and therapeutic areas are like merchant types or countries where transactions occur.

Needing to Clean the Data

Many longitudinal databases—clinical, financial, or both—were created to collect information from clinical staff using drop-down lists for patient management. This results in data that includes common mismatches, where very different items have similar names as well as data values that should be, but are not, compulsory. The lack of internal data checking can also give rise to anomalies that are not necessarily critical with regard to patient management but that add to the complexity of the analysis when data is processed for epidemiological studies:

- Gender can be recorded as male, female, or unknown.

- Medical events and prescriptions can have associated dates before the practice registration date, or after the date of death.

- Prostate cancer and other male-specific conditions can be recorded for females.

- Hysterectomy and other female-specific conditions can be recorded for males.

Depending on the analysis and data selection, you can correct these anomalies or remove the patients. However, most of the programming effort is spent specifying codes to identify the medical conditions or prescription drugs of interest.

Choosing a Suitable Database

Databases have different characteristics (geographical location, age profile, duration of patient registration, and so on), and no single database includes the data required for every study in epidemiology. Therefore, which database(s) to select can be an important decision when you are designing a study. Here are some examples:

- GPRD, ffGPRD, and THIN – UK, GP records, 6m+ patients, representative age sample, average registration 7.5 years, updated monthly

- LifeLink – US, employee claims database, 1.8m patients, good elderly coverage and poor coverage of 25–34, average registration 6.9 years, no updates after Q1 2003

- IHCIS – US, managed care database, 20m patients, poor coverage of elderly, average registration 1.5 years, updated 6-monthly

Database selection must also consider which data items are available, because many databases do not contain all types of data:

- Outpatient and hospitalization records

- Laboratory data

- Smoking data

- Repeat prescriptions

- Height and weight data

- Death information

- Links between family members

- Links between medical events and prescriptions

The selection decision should also take into account the therapeutic area, because some databases have better representation of certain medical conditions due to their patient selection:

- LifeLink has better coverage of Type II diabetes than IHCIS due to the higher coverage of elderly patients.

- US databases include more data on certain drugs than UK databases due to very different prescribing patterns.

Programming Techniques

The simplest technique for a SAS programmer faced with large input data sets involves sorting the data after it has been reduced to a more manageable volume. The code examples in the following sections have been simplified to demonstrate the effect of increasing data volumes on elapsed time.

Sample Data Sets

I like to create sample data using SAS data sets readily available to SAS programmers. In this case, I have saved multiple copies of sashelp.cars into the main data set:

```
%LET mult = 1000; /*1, 10, 100, 1000, 2000, 5000, 10000*/

DATA main;
    SET sashelp.cars;
    DO i = 1 to &mult.;
        OUTPUT;
    END;
RUN;
```

Sample SAS Code

The macro variables created here can be used to modify the sample code shown in the following sections:

```
%LET vars = Make Model Type Origin Horsepower MPG_City MPG_Highway Weight;

%LET inkeep = KEEP = &vars.;
%LET outkeep = KEEP = &vars.;
%LET datakeep = KEEP = &vars.;
%LET setkeep = KEEP = &vars.;

%LET datawhere = WHERE = (type = 'Wagon');
%LET if = IF type = 'Wagon';
%LET setwhere = WHERE type = 'Wagon';
```

Following is a quick guide to where you can achieve performance savings:

- &inkeep and &setkeep reduce the volume of input data before processing and should be better than &outkeep and &datakeep, which reduce the volume of data output after processing.

- &setwhere selects data on input, which should be better than &if, which selects data after reading; and also better than &datawhere, which selects data on output after processing.

- The greatest gains should be made by reducing the data volume before any processing, so subsetting the data before sorting will show the most significant benefit.

PROC SORT before DATA Step Subset

The following code shows how you can modify the basic PROC SORT and DATA step statements using the macro variables to adjust program performance:

```
PROC SORT DATA = main (&inkeep.) OUT = outdsn (&outkeep.);
    BY origin make;
RUN;

DATA final (&datakeep. &datawhere.);
    SET outdsn (&setkeep.);
    &if.;
    &setwhere.;
RUN;
```

The following sections show the SAS code for which results are reported later, in Figure 3-1.

Code: sort_if

This is an unmodified PROC SORT step, followed by a DATA step subset using an IF statement:

```
PROC SORT DATA = main OUT = subset_sort10;
    BY origin make;
RUN;

DATA subset_sort11;
    SET subset_sort10;
    IF type = 'Wagon';
RUN;
```

Code: sort_setwhere

This is an unmodified PROC SORT step, followed by a DATA step subset using a WHERE statement:

```
PROC SORT DATA = main OUT = subset_sort10;
    BY origin make;
RUN;
```

```
DATA subset_sort12;
    SET subset_sort10;
    WHERE type = 'Wagon';
RUN;
```

Code: sort_outkeep_if

This is a PROC SORT step using a KEEP option on the output data set to reduce the number of variables, followed by a DATA step subset using an IF statement:

```
PROC SORT DATA = main OUT = subset_sort20 (keep = &vars.);
    BY origin make;
RUN;

DATA subset_sort21;
    SET subset_sort20;
    IF type = 'Wagon';
RUN;
```

Code: sort_outkeep_setwhere

This is a PROC SORT step using a KEEP option on the output data set to reduce the number of variables, followed by a DATA step subset using a WHERE statement:

```
PROC SORT DATA = main OUT = subset_sort20 (keep = &vars.);
    BY origin make;
RUN;

DATA subset_sort22;
    SET subset_sort20;
    WHERE type = 'Wagon';
RUN;
```

Code: sort_inkeep_if

This is a PROC SORT step using a KEEP option on the input data set to reduce the number of variables, followed by a DATA step subset using an IF statement:

```
PROC SORT DATA = main (keep = &vars.) OUT = subset_sort30;
    BY origin make;
RUN;

DATA subset_sort31;
    SET subset_sort30;
    IF type = 'Wagon';
RUN;
```

Code: sort_inkeep_setwhere

This is a PROC SORT step using a KEEP option on the input data set to reduce the number of variables, followed by a DATA step subset using a WHERE statement:

```
PROC SORT DATA = main (keep = &vars.) OUT = subset_sort30;
    BY origin make;
RUN;

DATA subset_sort32;
    SET subset_sort30;
    WHERE type = 'Wagon';
RUN;
```

PROC SORT after DATA Step Subset

The following code shows how you can modify the basic DATA step and PROC SORT statements using the macro variables to adjust program performance:

```
DATA datadsn (&datakeep. &datawhere.);
    SET main (&setkeep.);
    &if.;
    &setwhere.;
RUN;

PROC SORT DATA = datadsn (&inkeep.) OUT = final (&outkeep.);
    BY origin make;
RUN;
```

The following sections show the modified SAS code for which results are reported later, in Figures 3-1 and 3-2.

Code: if_sort

This is a DATA step subset using an IF statement, followed by an unmodified PROC SORT step:

```
DATA subset_sort40;
    SET main;
    IF type = 'Wagon';
RUN;

PROC SORT DATA = subset_sort40 OUT = subset_sort41;
    BY origin make;
RUN;
```

Code: setwhere_sort

This is a DATA step subset using a WHERE statement, followed by an unmodified PROC SORT step:

```
DATA subset_sort50;
    SET main;
    WHERE type = 'Wagon';
RUN;

PROC SORT DATA = subset_sort50 OUT = subset_sort51;
    BY origin make;
RUN;
```

Code: datawhere_sort

This is a DATA step subset using a WHERE clause on the output data set, followed by an unmodified PROC SORT step:

```
DATA subset_sort60 (WHERE = (type = 'Wagon'));
    SET main;
RUN;

PROC SORT DATA = subset_sort60 OUT = subset_sort61;
    BY origin make;
RUN;
```

Code: setwhere_setkeep_sort

This is a DATA step subset with a WHERE statement, using a KEEP option on the input data set to reduce the number of variables, followed by an unmodified PROC SORT step:

```
DATA subset_sort80;
    SET main (keep = &vars.);
    WHERE type = 'Wagon';
RUN;

PROC SORT DATA = subset_sort80 OUT = subset_sort81;
    BY origin make;
RUN;
```

Performance Results

The sashelp.cars data set has 428 observations and 16 variables. You can use the &vars macro variable to reduce the number of variables to 8. The number of observations in the main data set from the multiples of sashelp.cars are as follows:

- ×1 = 428

- ×10 = 4,280

- ×100 = 42,800

- ×1,000 = 428,000

- ×2,000 = 856,000

- ×5,000 = 2,140,000

- ×10,000 = 4,280,000

In Figures 3-1 and 3-2, the differences between the elapsed times of the different SAS programs becomes more obvious with greater than 5,000 copies of sashelp.cars (that is, more than 2,140,000 records) in the main data set, which is significantly larger than most SAS data sets used in clinical trials but typical of those found in epidemiology. In particular, there is a definite separation of elapsed times between those programs where sorting is completed first and those where sorting is completed after the subset.

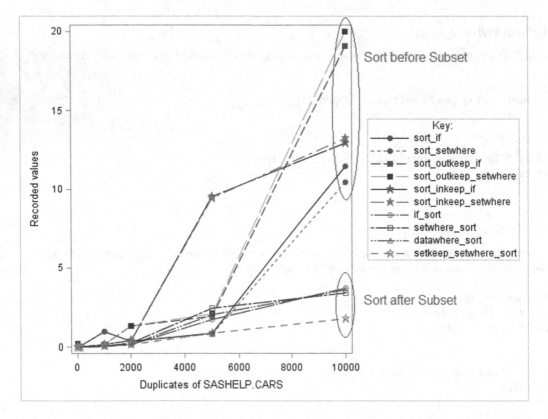

Figure 3-1. *Elapsed time of programs including subset and sort steps, showing the benefit of sorting after the subset*

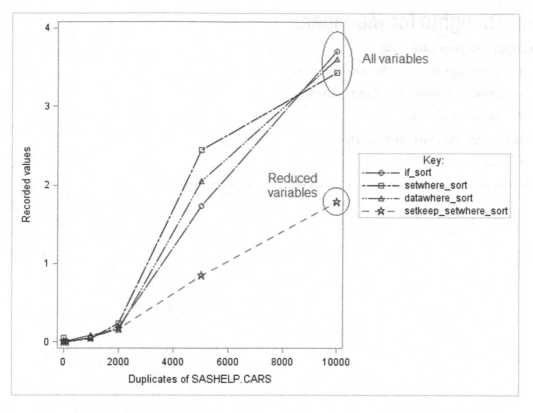

Figure 3-2. *Elapsed time for programs where the subset completed before sorting, showing the benefit of dropping unnecessary variables*

Figure 3-2 looks in more detail at SAS programs where sorting is performed on the subset data. Elapsed times are quite small, so it is difficult to infer very much from these figures, but it appears that reducing the number of variables read into the DATA step and PROC SORT further improves the elapsed time.

Summary

SAS programmers in epidemiology may need to be able to cope with the following situations:

- Processing massive amounts of data

- Cleaning input data so that it is consistent, which is not often done as part of data management

- Developing coding lists for medical events and prescriptions, which again is not done as part of data management

- Selecting an appropriate database for each protocol

- Adapting SAS code to cope with databases' different data content and structures

Some Thoughts for Managers

Epidemiology data processing is like

- Detecting fraud in credit card transactions
- Selecting customers for direct marketing
- Analyzing web logs

Epidemiology data processing is *not* like

- Clinical trials

Who should at least be interviewed for epidemiology data-processing jobs?

PART II

■ ■ ■

External Interfaces

Overview

In every development project, there are interfaces between SAS and external applications. This part of the book examines how SAS can communicate, directly or indirectly, with external applications:

- Chapter 4, "SAS to R to SAS," demonstrates how to use R to create images for a SAS report, as well as how other external applications can be interfaced with SAS.

- Chapter 5, "Knit Perl and SAS for DIY Web Applications," gives an example of how you can use Perl to create an interactive web interface to a SAS program.

- Chapter 6, "Running SAS Programs in Enterprise Guide," demonstrates how to set up Enterprise Guide to run collections of SAS programs (for example, for clinical trials).

- Chapter 7, "Running SAS Programs in SAS Studio or Enterprise Guide," compares three interactive user interfaces to SAS: Display Manager (the interactive part of SAS software), Enterprise Guide (a front-end application for Windows, written in .NET), and SAS Studio (a front-end web application written in Java).

- Chapter 8, "Everyday Uses for SAS Output Delivery System (ODS)," explains how to create external file formats suitable for Microsoft Office, OpenOffice. org, LibreOffice, and Adobe Reader.

■ ■ ■

## CHAPTER 4

SAS to R to SAS

The aim of this chapter is to describe one method of passing SAS data from SAS to R, using R to produce a graph, and then passing that graph back to SAS for inclusion in an ODS document. The R programming language provides a wide range of graphical functionality, some of which is unavailable or time-consuming to achieve in SAS—either in SAS/GRAPH or ODS Graphics. The method described here makes this functionality available to SAS applications. You can also adapt these basic principles to create character-based reports using R for inclusion in SAS reports.

Software Environment

This chapter includes the following software configurations and methods are described in this chapter:

- The examples use Windows, but you can use any platform compatible with SAS and R. Unix and Linux file-naming conventions would require you to rename the files passed between SAS and R.

- The techniques can be used in any version of Base SAS from version 7 onward. No other licensed SAS components are required.

- R requires two nonstandard add-on libraries to be installed to support the techniques used in this chapter. The Hmisc library adds R functions to import foreign data into R (SAS data, comma-separated value (CSV) data, and so on). This library requires an additional SAS macro, %exportlib, which can be used to export a folder of SAS data sets into a collection of CSV files to be read into R using the sasxport. get function. The lattice library adds R functions to create trellis graphics. In addition, the grDevices library is supplied as part of the R system and includes functions to create a variety of image file formats, including JPEG, GIF, and PNG.

Program Flow

The program flow covers both SAS and R activities. The following SAS code shown in this section creates a sample SAS data set from the SAS-supplied sashelp.prdsale data set. This data set is processed using the %exportlib macro to create CSV (comma-separated values) text files which that can be read by R. The SAS program then writes the R code that will generate the lattice of plots in a JPEG image files, which will ultimately be included in an ODS report.

SAS Activity to Prepare the Data

The first step in the SAS activity involves selecting an SAS data set to transfer and saving the data set to a folder, as follows:

```
LIBNAME new 'c:\temp\new';

PROC datasets LIB=new KILL;
RUN;
QUIT;

DATA sasuser.v_prdsale / VIEW = sasuser.v_prdsale;
  SET sashelp.prdsale;
  LENGTH yyq $6;
  yyqtr = year + (quarter - 1)/4;
  mon = MONTH(month);
  yyq = PUT(month, YYQ6.);
  yq = INTCK('QTR', '31dec1992'd, month);
  SELECT (country);
    WHEN ('U.S.A.') cntry = 'USA';
    WHEN ('GERMANY') cntry = 'DE';
    WHEN ('CANADA') cntry = 'CA';
    OTHERWISE;
  END;
RUN;

PROC SUMMARY DATA = sasuser.v_prdsale MISSING NWAY;
  CLASS cntry yq product;
  VAR actual;
  OUTPUT OUT = new.prdsale SUM =;
RUN;
```

Next, you export the folder to CSV files (using %exportlib), including the contents of the folder and any SAS user formats. Note that the folders must be written with '/' separators even if you are running the program in Windows. The macro exports all SAS data sets in a data library to CSV files. One of the data sets is assumed to be the result of PROC FORMAT CNTLOUT= if any user formats are referenced.

Numeric variables are formatted in BEST16. format so that date/time variables are exported with their internal numeric values. A special file, _contents_.csv, is created to hold, for all data sets combined, the data set name, data set label, variable names, labels, formats, types, and lengths. The code is expressed as follows:

```
/* Macro exportlib
Usage:
  %exportlib(lib, outdir, tempdir);

Arguments:
  lib     - SAS libname for input data sets
  outdir  - directory in which to write .csv files
            (default ".")
  tempdir - temporary directory to hold generated SAS code
            (default C:/WINDOWS/TEMP)
*/
```

```
%MACRO exportlib(lib, outdir, tempdir);
  %IF %QUOTE(&outdir.) = %THEN %LET outdir = .;
  %IF %QUOTE(&tempdir.) = %THEN %LET tempdir = C:/WINDOWS/TEMP;

  OPTIONS NOFMTERR;

  PROC COPY IN = &lib. OUT = work;
  RUN;

  PROC CONTENTS DATA = work._ALL_ NOPRINT
    OUT=_contents_(KEEP = memname memlabel name type label
                            format length nobs);
  RUN;

  PROC EXPORT DATA = _contents_
              OUTFILE = "&outdir./_contents_.csv" REPLACE;
  RUN;

  DATA _NULL_;
    SET _contents_;
    BY memname;
    FILE "&tempdir/_export_.sas";
    RETAIN bk -1;
    IF FIRST.memname AND (nobs > 0) THEN DO;
      PUT 'DATA ' memname ';';
      PUT '  SET ' memname ';';
      PUT '  FORMAT _NUMERIC_ BEST14.;';
      PUT 'RUN;';
      PUT 'PROC EXPORT DATA = ' memname;
      PUT '              OUTFILE = "'
          "&outdir./" memname +bk '.csv"';
      PUT '              REPLACE;';
      PUT 'RUN;';
    END;
  RUN;

  %INCLUDE "&tempdir./_export_.sas";
%MEND exportlib;

PROC FORMAT CNTLOUT = _cntlout;
RUN;

%exportlib(new, c:/temp/r, c:/windows/temp);
```

Next, generate the R code (including sasxport.get) to read CSV files and write the generated graph to a JPEG file of 480 × 480 pixels:

```
DATA _NULL_;
  FILE 'c:\temp\r\program.r' LRECL = 1024;
  PUT 'library(Hmisc)';
  PUT 'library(lattice)';
```

43

```
  PUT 'library(grDevices)';
  PUT "sasdata <- sasxport.get('c:/temp/r', method=('csv'))";
  PUT "trellis.device(jpeg, file='c:/temp/r/program.jpg',";
  PUT '                width=480, height=480)';
  PUT 'trellis.par.set(theme=col.whitebg())';
  PUT "trellis.par.set('background',list(col='white'))";
  PUT "trellis.par.set('plot.symbol',list(col='blue'))";
  PUT "trellis.par.set('dot.symbol',list(col='blue'))";
  PUT "trellis.par.set('axis.line',list(col='red'))";
  PUT "trellis.par.set('box.rectangle',list(col='red'))";
  PUT "trellis.par.set('par.xlab.text',list(col='green'))";
  PUT "trellis.par.set('par.ylab.text',list(col='green'))";
  PUT "trellis.par.set('par.zlab.text',list(col='green'))";
  PUT "trellis.par.set('axis.text',list(col='green'))";
  PUT 'xyplot(actual ~ yq | product*cntry';
  PUT '        ,data=sasdata$prdsale';
  PUT "        ,xlab = 'Quarter'";
  PUT "        ,ylab = 'Actual Sales'";
  PUT '        ,panel = function(x, y) {';
  PUT '                    panel.grid(h=-1, v=-1)';
  PUT '                    panel.xyplot(x, y)';
  PUT '                    panel.loess(x, y';
  PUT '                             ,span=1';
  PUT '                             ,degree=2';
  PUT '                             )';
  PUT '                   }';
  PUT "        ,main = 'Plotted using R'";
  PUT '        )';
  PUT 'dev.off()';
  PUT 'q()';
RUN;
```

Execute the R command line, including the R code file as the input program. In this case, you can find the R program in the Windows default program path:

```
OPTIONS XWAIT XSYNC;
X "r.exe --no-save --quiet <""c:\temp\r\program.r""
                     >""c:\temp\r\program.log""";
```

R Activity

Executing R code involves outputting the R log to a text file and the graph to a JPEG file. Note that the white background is required for most ODS styles to allow the resulting graphs to coordinate with their color schemes. The default background for R graphs is a light gray:

```
library(Hmisc)
library(lattice)
library(grDevices)

sasdata <- sasxport.get('c:/temp/r', method=('csv'))
```

44

```
trellis.device(jpeg, file='c:/temp/r/program.jpg',
               width=480, height=480)
trellis.par.set(theme=col.whitebg())
trellis.par.set('background',list(col='white'))
trellis.par.set('plot.symbol',list(col='blue'))
trellis.par.set('dot.symbol',list(col='blue'))
trellis.par.set('axis.line',list(col='red'))
trellis.par.set('box.rectangle',list(col='red'))
trellis.par.set('par.xlab.text',list(col='green'))
trellis.par.set('par.ylab.text',list(col='green'))
trellis.par.set('axis.text',list(col='green'))

xyplot(actual ~ yq | product*cntry
      ,data=sasdata$prdsale
      ,xlab = 'Quarter'
      ,ylab = 'Actual Sales'
      ,panel = function(x, y) {
                          panel.grid(h=-1, v=-1)
                          panel.xyplot(x, y)
                          panel.loess(x, y
                                     ,span=1
                                     ,degree=2
                                     )
                          }
      ,main = 'Plotted using R'
      )
dev.off()
```

Close R session:

```
q()
```

SAS Activity to Create the ODS Report

For the next SAS activity, open the ODS destination, such as HTML

```
ODS ESCAPECHAR = '^';
ODS HTML FILE = 'c:\temp\r\report.html' STYLE = minimal
        GPATH = 'c:\temp\r' GTITLE GFOOTNOTE;
```

or RTF:

```
ODS ESCAPECHAR = '^';
ODS RTF FILE = 'c:\temp\r\report.rtf' STYLE = minimal
        GTITLE GFOOTNOTE;
```

Incorporate the JPEG file in the SAS report in HTML

```
DATA _NULL_;
  FILE PRINT;
```

45

```
  PUT "<IMG SRC='c:\temp\r\program.jpg' BORDER='0'>";
RUN;
```

or RTF:

```
DATA _NULL_;
  FILE PRINT;
  PUT "^S={PREIMAGE='c:\temp\r\program.jpg'}";
RUN;
```

Finally, close the ODS destination:

```
ODS _ALL_ CLOSE;
```

The lattice image created by R is shown in Figure 4-1. Figure 4-2 shows the corresponding image included in an ODS HTML report using SAS.

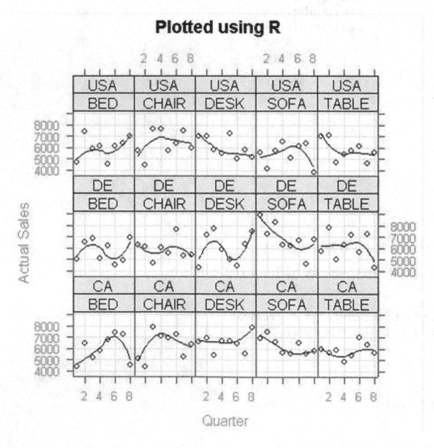

Figure 4-1. *Lattice image created by R*

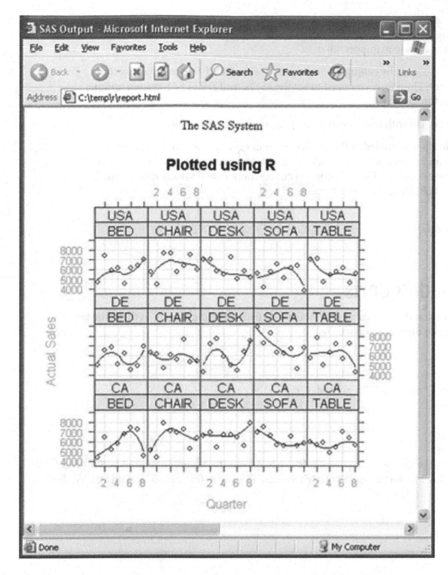

Figure 4-2. *The same image incorporated into an HTML page using SAS ODS*

Coding Issues

As an experienced SAS programmer but an inexperienced R programmer, I had to resolve the following issues while developing this reporting application:

- HTML reports require a different syntax for displaying external image files than that used for non-HTML reports, (e.g., RTF, PDF, and so on), so the code must include separate code sections for use with HTML and non-HTML destinations.

- Because different output destinations have different acceptable image formats, you need try to select an image format that is compatible with for all the expected output destinations.

- Because the export processing creates CSV files for every SAS data set in the specified folder, limiting the number of SAS data sets in that folder will reduce the run time required for the R code to import the data.

- The R code is executed by calling the R system in -command-line mode using the SAS X statement. Therefore, you need to set the XSYNC and XWAIT SAS system options must be set before calling R.

- R programs may fail with minimal error information in the R log file.

- If SAS/IML Studio is installed and the RLANG system option is set on session start, then R code can be incorporated in SAS programs. You can test for the presence of the RLANG system option with the following code, where RLANG means R code can be included, and NORLANG means that it cannot:

```
PROC OPTIONS OPTION=RLANG;
RUN;
```

Character-Based Reports

Most R statistical functions can direct their output to text files instead of the screen, in the same way graphical functions can write directly to image files:

```
library(Hmisc)

sasdata <- sasxport.get('c:/temp/r', method=('csv'))
attach(sasdata$prdsale)
sink('program.txt')
summary(sasdata$prdsale)
```

You can use SAS code like the following to include the text from the report generated in R into an ODS report in SAS. Remembering to select an ODS style where that allows the text can to be read against the report background:

```
DATA _NULL_;
  INFILE 'program.txt';
  FILE PRINT;
  INPUT;
  PUT _INFILE_;
RUN;
```

Conclusions

The example given in this chapter is not the only way to link SAS with external applications, but it demonstrates that it is possible for SAS to make use of the strengths of suitable external software.

Software Resources and Further Reading

- R Project for Statistical Computing: www.r-project.org

- %exportlib: http://biostat.mc.vanderbilt.edu/twiki/pub/Main/Hmisc/
exportlib.sas

- Base SAS Focus Area, https://support.sas.com/rnd/base/index.html.

■ ■ ■

## CHAPTER 5

Knit Perl and SAS Software for DIY Web Applications

If your organization develops a web-based SAS application for 30+ users, then the logical choice is to use SAS/IntrNet software, due to its speed, reliability, and cost-effectiveness. However, if your entire organization has fewer than 30 employees, is there a cost-effective alternative to SAS/IntrNet software that still allows access to SAS-based data?

The answer is yes—there are a number of possible solutions. For example, by combining a client license for Base SAS software, a web server application, a simple application dispatcher written in Perl, and a knowledge of HTML, it is possible to write SAS code and HTML to provide drill-down reports on SAS-based data to users with access only to a web browser.

This chapter demonstrates some of the techniques available to SAS programmers to generate drill-down applications for web browsers.

HTML Programming

The core of this simple drill-down web application is the HTML FORM, which allows the user to select the data hierarchies to use across the top and down the side of the generated report. The drop-down lists used to subset the data, which are generated later from the available data, should be hard-coded or omitted in the initial HTML code, depending on your individual needs.

The two hidden INPUT tags, _program and _grafics, are required by the Perl server application to tell it where the SAS code is located and whether to generate a text web page or a single graphics image, respectively. All other INPUT and SELECT tags create SAS macro variables in the generated SAS code.

The initial HTML code is regenerated by the SAS code in the left column of the two-column HTML TABLE, with the report placed in the column on the right.

The web page used to send the initial web request forms the basis of the left column of the drill-down reports. You see this HTML in the SAS code later in this chapter:

```
<HTML><HEAD>
 <TITLE>
  Generation of a Web-based Report from a SAS v9 Application
 </TITLE>
</HEAD>
```

```html
<BODY>
 <CENTER><TABLE CELLPADDING=5>
  <TR><TD BGCOLOR="ffffc0">

   <FORM ACTION="../cgi-bin/new-sas9.pl" METHOD=POST>
    <INPUT TYPE=HIDDEN NAME="_program" VALUE="code.drill9.sas">
    <INPUT TYPE=HIDDEN NAME="_grafics" VALUE="n">
    <BR>Report title?<BR>
    <INPUT TYPE=TEXT NAME="title" VALUE="Title" SIZE=25><BR>

    <HR><BR>Select country?<BR>
    <SELECT NAME=country>
     <OPTION VALUE=" " SELECTED> <BR>
     <OPTION VALUE="CANADA">CANADA <BR>
     <OPTION VALUE="GERMANY">GERMANY <BR>
     <OPTION VALUE="U.S.A.">U.S.A. <BR>
    </SELECT><BR>

    <INPUT NAME=down TYPE=RADIO VALUE="1" CHECKED>Down  
    <INPUT NAME=across TYPE=RADIO VALUE="1">Across<BR>

    <HR><BR>Select division?<BR>
    <SELECT NAME=division>
     <OPTION VALUE=" " SELECTED> <BR>
     <OPTION VALUE="CONSUMER">CONSUMER <BR>
     <OPTION VALUE="EDUCATION">EDUCATION <BR>
    </SELECT><BR>

    <INPUT NAME=down TYPE=RADIO VALUE="2">Down  
    <INPUT NAME=across TYPE=RADIO VALUE="2">Across<BR>

    <HR><BR>Select year?<BR>
    <SELECT NAME=year>
     <OPTION VALUE=" " SELECTED> <BR>
     <OPTION VALUE="1993">1993 <BR>
     <OPTION VALUE="1994">1994 <BR>
    </SELECT><BR>

    <INPUT NAME=down TYPE=RADIO VALUE="3">Down  
    <INPUT NAME=across TYPE=RADIO VALUE="3" CHECKED>Across<BR>

    <HR>
    <INPUT TYPE=SUBMIT VALUE="Generate Report">
   </FORM>
  </TD></TR>
 </TABLE></CENTER>
</BODY></HTML>
```

52

System Requirements

A number of system requirements must be fulfilled by both the server and the client in this application. Server requirements include the following:

- Windows XP/Vista/7/8 or UNIX/Linux operating system software running on a server platform with sufficient processing power, memory, and disk space to run multiple SAS software sessions

- Web server software, such as Apache, Microsoft IIS, Xitami, or similar

- Base SAS version 8 or 9 software installed on the web server

- Perl software version 5.002 or above installed on the web server

The client requires web browser software, such as Internet Explorer, Mozilla Firefox, Google Chrome, Safari, Opera, or similar.

SAS Programming

The SAS code uses SAS macro variables passed to it by the Perl-generated SAS program to subset and summarize the SAS data and to regenerate the HTML web page for the next selection:

```
* Program : Drill9.sas                              *;
* Comments: Generate web page with drill-down facility for the  *;
*           SASHELP.PRDSALE SAS dataset:             *;
*             Analysis=ACTUAL                        *;
*             Geographic=COUNTRY - U.S.A./GERMANY/CANADA  *;
*                        REGION - EAST/WEST          *;
*             Product=DIVISION - CONSUMER/EDUCATION  *;
*                     PRODTYPE - OFFICE/FURNITURE    *;
*                     PRODUCT - SOFA/BED/TABLE/DESK/CHAIR  *;
*             Date=YEAR - 1993/1994                  *;
*                  QUARTER - 1/2/3/4                 *;
*                  MONTH - Jan/Feb/.../Nov/Dec       *;
```

Make sure all the expected macro variables exist and are global before opening the macro:

```
%GLOBAL country region division prodtype product year quarter
        month down across title;
%LET analysis=actual;
```

Select the output file reference to be used, along with the table colors:

```
%LET fileref=_webout;
%LET leftcol=ffffc0;  /* yellow */
%LET rightcol=c0c0ff;  /* blue */
%LET cellcol=ffffff;  /* white */
```

Find the path and filename of the physical output file specified by the &fileref macro variable using the DICTIONARY views in SASHELP. This path and filename allow the code to be split up the production of HTMLover several steps:

```
DATA _NULL_;
    SET sashelp.vextfl (WHERE=(fileref=UPCASE("&fileref.")));
    PUT 'FILENAME=' fileref ', XPATH=' xpath;
    CALL SYMPUT('extpath',TRIM(LEFT(xpath)));
    STOP;
RUN;
```

Start the drill macro definition:

```
%MACRO drill;
```

Assign the report title:

```
TITLE1 "&title. ";
```

Set default values for the hierarchies and selections:

```
%DO i=1 %TO 8;
    %LET c&i.=;
%END;

%LET flag=0;
%LET class1=country;
%LET class2=division;
%LET class3=year;
```

Update the country hierarchy and selection based on the &country and &region macro variable values provided from the HTML FORM:

```
%IF %SUBSTR(&country.,1,1) NE %THEN %DO;
    %LET c1=country=%STR(%'&country.%');
    %LET flag=1;
    %LET class1=region;
%END;

%IF %SUBSTR(&region.,1,1) NE %THEN %DO;
    %IF &flag.=1 %THEN %DO;
        %LET c2=%STR(%'&region.%');
    %END;
    %ELSE %DO;
        %LET c2=%STR(region=%'&region.%');
    %END;
    %LET flag=1;
    %LET class1=region;
%END;
```

Update the product hierarchy and selection based on the &division, &prodtype, and &product macro variable values provided from the HTML FORM:

```
%IF %SUBSTR(&division.,1,1) NE %THEN %DO;
    %IF &flag.=1 %THEN %DO;
        %LET c3=%STR(AND division=%'&division.%');
    %END;
    %ELSE %DO;
        %LET c3=%STR(division=%'&division.%');
    %END;
    %LET flag=1;
    %LET class2=prodtype;
%END;

%IF %SUBSTR(&prodtype.,1,1) NE %THEN %DO;
    %IF &flag.=1 %THEN %DO;
        %LET c4=%STR(AND prodtype=%'&prodtype.%');
    %END;
    %ELSE %DO;
        %LET c4=%STR(prodtype=%'&prodtype.%');
    %END;
    %LET flag=1;
    %LET class2=product;
%END;

%IF %SUBSTR(&product.,1,1) NE %THEN %DO;
    %IF &flag.=1 %THEN %DO;
        %LET c5=%STR(AND product=%'&product.%');
    %END;
    %ELSE %DO;
        %LET c5=%STR(product=%'&product.%');
    %END;
    %LET flag=1;
    %LET class2=product;
%END;
```

Update the date hierarchy and selection based on the &year, &quarter, and &month macro variable values provided from the HTML FORM:

```
%IF %SUBSTR(&year.,1,1) NE %THEN %DO;
    %IF &flag.=1 %THEN %DO;
        %LET c6=AND year=&year.;
    %END;
    %ELSE %DO;
        %LET c6=year=&year.;
    %END;
    %LET flag=1;
    %LET class3=quarter;
%END;
```

```
%IF %SUBSTR(&quarter.,1,1) NE %THEN %DO;
    %IF &flag.=1 %THEN %DO;
        %LET c7=AND quarter=&quarter.;
    %END;
    %ELSE %DO;
        %LET c7=quarter=&quarter.;
    %END;
    %LET flag=1;
    %LET class3=month;
%END;

%IF %SUBSTR(&month.,1,1) NE %THEN %DO;
    %IF &flag.=1 %THEN %DO;
        %LET c8=%STR(AND month=%'&month.%');
    %END;
    %ELSE %DO;
        %LET c8=%STR(month=%'&month.%');
    %END;
    %LET flag=1;
    %LET class3=month;
%END;
```

Amalgamate the selections, and create a subset of the data:

```
%LET c0=%UNQUOTE(&c1. &c2. &c3. &c4. &c5. &c6. &c7. &c8.);

DATA selected;
    SET sashelp.prdsale
    %IF &flag.=1 %THEN %DO;
        (WHERE=(
                &c0.
                ))
    %END;
        ;
RUN;
```

Summarize the subset using the across and down hierarchies:

```
PROC SUMMARY DATA=selected NWAY;
    CLASS &&class&down. &&class&across.;
    VAR &analysis.;
    OUTPUT OUT=prdsumm SUM=;
RUN;
```

Create a list of hierarchy values for the drop-down selections on the web page, and count the values in each hierarchy:

```
%DO i=1 %TO 3;
    PROC SQL;
        CREATE TABLE values&i. AS
            SELECT DISTINCT
                    &&class&i.
            FROM   selected
            ORDER BY
                    &&class&i.
        ;
    QUIT;

    PROC SQL NOPRINT;
        SELECT COUNT(*)
        INTO   :nvalues&i.
        FROM   values&i.
        ;
    QUIT;
%END;
```

Write the HTML for the top of the web page to make sure all the ODS style information (the default style in this case) is included in the *top matter* (the HTML text at the top of any web page). Do not write any of the *bottom matter* HTML text at the end of the web page yet:

```
ODS LISTING CLOSE;
ODS HTML BODY=&fileref. (NO_BOTTOM_MATTER TITLE="&title.");

DATA _NULL_;
    FILE PRINT;
    PUT ' ';
RUN;

ODS HTML CLOSE;
```

Reassign the output destination to allow more HTML text to be appended:

```
FILENAME &fileref. "&extpath." MOD;
```

Start the outer table, with the submission form in the left table column:

```
DATA _NULL_;
    FILE &fileref.;
    PUT '<CENTER><TABLE CELLPADDING=5><TR><TD BGCOLOR="'
        "&leftcol." '">';

    PUT '<FORM ACTION="../cgi-bin/new-sas9.pl" METHOD=POST>';
    PUT '<INPUT TYPE=HIDDEN NAME="_program" VALUE="code.drill9.sas">';
    PUT '<INPUT TYPE=HIDDEN NAME="_grafics" VALUE="n">';
```

```
    %IF %SUBSTR(&country.,1,1) NE %THEN %DO;
        PUT '<INPUT TYPE=HIDDEN NAME=country VALUE="' "&country." '">';
    %END;

    %IF %SUBSTR(&division.,1,1) NE %THEN %DO;
        PUT '<INPUT TYPE=HIDDEN NAME=division VALUE="' "&division." '">';
    %END;

    %IF %SUBSTR(&prodtype.,1,1) NE %THEN %DO;
        PUT '<INPUT TYPE=HIDDEN NAME=prodtype VALUE="' "&prodtype." '">';
    %END;

    %IF %SUBSTR(&year.,1,1) NE %THEN %DO;
        PUT '<INPUT TYPE=HIDDEN NAME=year VALUE="' "&year." '">';
    %END;

    %IF %SUBSTR(&quarter.,1,1) NE %THEN %DO;
        PUT '<INPUT TYPE=HIDDEN NAME=quarter VALUE="' "&quarter." '">';
    %END;

    PUT '<BR>Report title?<BR>';
    PUT '<INPUT TYPE=TEXT NAME=title VALUE="'
        "&title." '" SIZE=25><BR>';
    PUT '<HR>';
    STOP;
RUN;
```

Create selection lists for the hierarchies:

```
DATA _NULL_;
    FILE &fileref.;
    %DO i=1 %TO 3;
        DO i=1 TO &&nvalues&i;
            SET values&i. POINT=i;
            FILE &fileref.;

            IF i = 1 THEN DO;
                PUT "<BR>Select &&class&i.?<BR>";
                PUT '<SELECT NAME=' "&&class&i." '>';
                PUT '<OPTION VALUE=" " SELECTED> <BR>';
            END;
            PUT '<OPTION VALUE="' &&class&i. +(-1) '">' &&class&i. '<BR>';

            IF i = &&nvalues&i. THEN DO;
                PUT '</SELECT><BR>';
                PUT '<INPUT NAME=down TYPE=RADIO VALUE="' "&i." '"'

                %IF &i. = &down. %THEN %DO;
                    ' CHECKED'
                %END;
                    '>Down  ';
                PUT '<INPUT NAME=across TYPE=RADIO VALUE="' "&i." '"'
```

```
                    %IF &i. = &across. %THEN %DO;
                          ' CHECKED'
                    %END;
                          '>Across<BR><HR>';
                END;
             END;
        %END;
        STOP;
RUN;
```

End the submission form and left table column, and start the right table column:

```
DATA _NULL_;
    FILE &fileref.;
    PUT '<INPUT TYPE=HIDDEN NAME="_program" VALUE="code.drill9.sas">';
    PUT '<INPUT TYPE=HIDDEN NAME="_grafics" VALUE="n">';
    PUT '<INPUT TYPE=SUBMIT VALUE="Generate SAS v9 Report">';
    PUT '</FORM>';
    PUT '</TD><TD BGCOLOR="' "&rightcol." '">';
    STOP;
RUN;
```

Create the report using PROC TABULATE and ODS. There is no need to specify an ODS style here, because the style information has already been recorded in the HTML header (*top matter*). You still do not want to write any of the *bottom matter* HTML text at the end of the web page:

```
ODS HTML BODY=&fileref. (NO_TOP_MATTER NO_BOTTOM_MATTER);

PROC TABULATE DATA=selected;
    CLASS &&class&down. &&class&across.;
    VAR &analysis.;
    TABLE &&class&down., &&class&across. * actual*F=COMMA13.2;
    TITLE "&title. ";
    TITLE2 "&co. ";
    KEYLABEL N=' ' SUM=' ';
RUN;

ODS HTML CLOSE;
```

Finally, you can end the web page HTML by closing the TABLE and BODY sections. This is effectively the *bottom matter*, which complete s the web page:

```
DATA _NULL_;
    FILE &fileref.;
    PUT '</TD></TR></TABLE></CENTER>';
    PUT '</BODY>';
    PUT '</HTML>';
    STOP;
RUN;
```

End the drill macro definition, execute it, and clear the output file reference:

```
%MEND drill;

%drill;

FILENAME &fileref. CLEAR;
```

Perl Programming and Operational Details

Following are some sample user modifications to the header of the Perl server application to run SAS programs in SAS 9.2 on Windows:

```
print "HTTP/1.0 200 OK\n";

#! c:\perl\bin\perl.exe -w
# File name: c:\httpd\cgi-bin\...
# ...new-sas9.pl
#
# USER Modification begins here
#
# If running on Window, set 1; UNIX, set 0.
$OS_WIN= 1; ## If Windows, set 1.

# Directory for SAS to use for temporary files
$HOME= 'e:\\web_server\\temp';

# File containing libref & directory name pairs
$CONF= 'e:\\web_server\\cgi-bin\\new-sas9-perl.cfg';

# This is the full path name of the SAS System.
$SAS_EXE= 'c:\\progra~1\\sas\\sasfou~1\\9.2\\sas.exe -nologo';

# SAS options
$OPTIONS= '';

#
# End of USER Modification
#
```

The Perl server application, which was written by Michael Yu, needs to be customized before it can be called from a web page (discussed earlier):

- $OS_WIN indicates whether the web server is on a Windows or UNIX platform; they have different file-naming conventions.

- $HOME is the server directory, which holds the temporary files created by each web request.

- $CONF is the parameter file (shown in a moment) containing the pointers to directories on the server required by the processing.

- $SAS_EXE is the command line used to execute the SAS system on the server.

- $OPTIONS can be used for any relevant SAS options, although none are required for this program.

Here is a sample Perl server application parameter file:

```
#
# File name: new-sas9-perl.cfg
#
# A line starting with pound sign, '#', or blank is a comment line.
# Typically place this file in the web server machine's CGI-BIN directory
#
# Syntax:
# a-SAS-fileref!physical-directory-existing-on-the-Web-server-machine
# Note the use of exclamation mark, '!', as separator
```

code!e:\web_server\code

web!e:\web_server\wwwroot

Figure 5-1 shows the web page used to generate the initial web request.

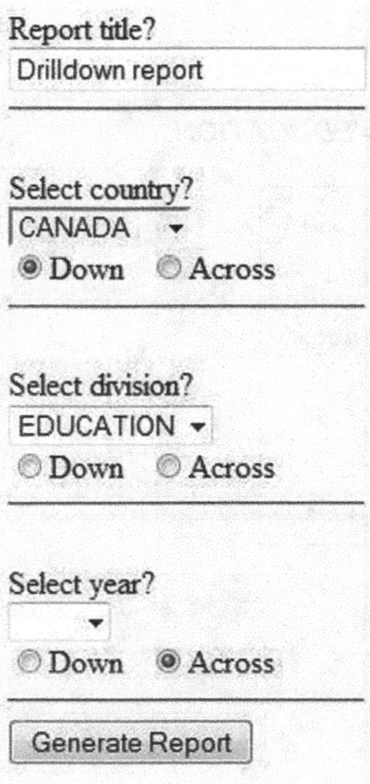

Figure 5-1. *The initial HTML web page*

The initial HTML web page calls the Perl server application used to generate a short SAS program (shown next), which contains the following:

- SAS macro variables corresponding to the FORM variables from the web page
- FILENAME statement pointing the _WEBOUT file reference to the HTML output file
- %INC statement pointing to the SAS program on the server to be executed

Here is the sample SAS program generated by the Perl server application:

```
%LET year= ;
%LET title=Drilldown report;
%LET country=CANADA;
%LET division=EDUCATION;
%LET down=1;
%LET across=3;

TITLE ; footnote ;

filename _WEBOUT 'e:\web_server\temp\p-2074705.out';

%inc 'e:\web_server\code\drill9.sas';
```

The web page report generated using SAS version 9.2 software and the default ODS style is shown in Figure 5-2.

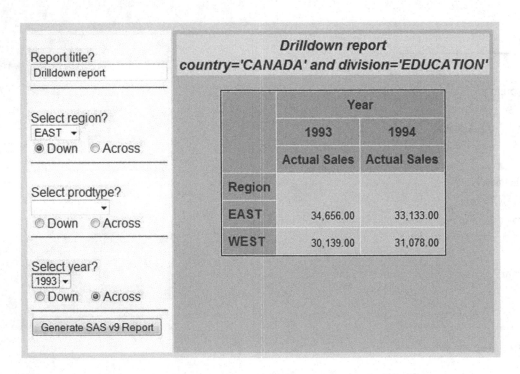

Figure 5-2. *The generated web page report with the filter options on the left side*

Conclusions

This very simple application has been developed to demonstrate the capabilities of the web interface to SAS. It returns dynamically created web reports on SAS-based data.

References

- Base SAS Focus Area, `https://support.sas.com/rnd/base/index.html`.

- Michael Yu, "Perl to SAS," `SUGICD.ZIP` (from the SUGI 24 CD_ROM Proceedings), and is included in the source code for this chapter.

CHAPTER 6

■ ■ ■

Running SAS Programs in Enterprise Guide

Geographical distribution of SAS programming teams across continents and oceans impacts access to study programs and data. It is only practical for local programmers to use direct GUI access to files, and remote programmers are forced to use copies of files on their local systems to achieve fast access. With Enterprise Guide (EG), because executed code and data are located on the designated server but files are viewed and edited on the local PC, network traffic is dramatically lessened, thus reducing the impact of remote working. This chapter describes the steps needed to use EG instead of batch SAS to run server-based study programs from anywhere in the world.

Environment Setup

When a SAS session is started on the server using EG, the current folder used is always the user's home folder by default: C:\WINDOWS\System32, /home/*user*, and so on. To change the current folder to a study-specific location, you can use the following SAS code:

```
%SYSEXEC cd
        /filespace/product/indication/studynumber/analysis/final/tables/programs;
%SYSEXEC setenv PWD
        /filespace/product/indication/studynumber/analysis/final/tables/programs;
```

Any automatic initialization programs that calculate locations based on the current path can now be able to set all the study-specific macro variables and allocate the library and filename references.

If you are using an autoexec.sas program to set the study-specific macro variables and allocate the library and filename references, it must be started here, too:

```
%INCLUDE 'autoexec.sas' / SOURCE2;
```

Changes to the Automatic Initialization Program

The only change required to the automatic initialization program is to alter the way the program name is obtained. In batch SAS sessions, the program name forms part of the SYSPROCESSNAME macro variable, (such as Program report.sas). However, when submitted from EG, the SYSPROCESSNAME macro variable in the SAS session always contains Object Server, with no program name. Fortunately, the label of the EG code node is stored in the _EGTASKLABEL macro variable. This label can be any string, until the code is saved to disk; once saved, it is replaced by the name of the saved file.

For example, you can replace this

```
%LET pgm = %SCAN(&sysprocessname., 2, %STR( ));
```

with this:

```
%IF "&sysprocessname." = "Object Server"
  %THEN %LET pgm = &_egtasklabel.;
  %ELSE %LET pgm = %SCAN(&sysprocessname., 2, %STR( ));
```

The code change in this automatic initialization program uses the _EGTASKLABEL macro variable instead of the SYSPROCESSNAME macro variable, but only if SYSPROCESSNAME contains Object Server, so batch SAS sessions are not impacted.

Limitations of Enterprise Guide Software

Because EG software acts as an editor and batch scheduler for separate SAS systems, it cannot be used to run SAS applications that have their own GUI interfaces or interactive features (SAS/AF, SAS/EIS, SAS/GIS, and so on). All processes should be considered batch jobs in that they have no interactive facilities. However, the SAS code is actually running in a single SAS session on the selected SAS server, so from the first code submission, WORK data sets, option settings, and macro variables are retained until the end of the server session, or until they are manually deleted. The batch SAS processes can only return the following items back to EG:

- SAS log

- SAS output via ODS

- SAS-generated graphs

Although the EG user interface includes elements relating to Base SAS, SAS/STAT, SAS/GRAPH, SAS/ETS, and SAS/QC, their applicability depends on the SAS license installed on the SAS server selected to run the code.

Accessing Local SAS Installations

EG software can be used as a point-and-click front end to a locally installed SAS system. This requires the client SAS software to be installed on the Windows system, including the local version of SAS Integration Technologies, which is supplied as part of Base SAS. The only SAS component that must be licensed is Base SAS.

Accessing the locally installed SAS system may require it to be registered using the /REGSERVER option on SAS.EXE, if the installation has not been installed into the default location or if several different versions have been installed on the same PC. For automated installations, it is recommended that you carry out this registration even if the location is the default.

Accessing Server-Based SAS Installations

A remote SAS server requires only Base SAS and SAS Integration Technologies to be installed and licensed, although if SAS/STAT, SAS/GRAPH, SAS/ETS, and SAS/QC are installed and licensed on the server, code can be generated for them by EG using standard tasks. You can also use other components, but doing so requires direct coding in a SAS code node to be executed from EG.

The remote SAS server must be configured using the SAS Enterprise Guide Explorer, which you can access from EG by clicking Tools ➤ SAS Enterprise Guide Explorer. You can add new servers using the Server Wizard, which you start from within the SAS Enterprise Guide Explorer by clicking File ➤ New ➤ Server. Each new server definition requires the following information: server name (user-defined, but must be unique), connection protocol (probably IOM), host address (either URL or IP address), and port number of the Object Spawner on the remote server.

Why You Cannot Use Autoexec.sas

EG communicates with the SAS System via a special interface component called SAS Integration Technologies. Requests for SAS functionality are normally small and frequent, so starting a full SAS session each time would be wasteful and probably too slow. As a consequence, SAS Integration Technologies starts only a minimal system, which can be extended, if required, as the code is compiled. This minimal system does not include any autoexec processing, so any processing required to be carried out prior to each request must be initiated using the -INITSTMT option. Therefore, the following option is equivalent to the -AUTOEXEC option:

```
-INITSTMT '%INCLUDE "/home/user/autoexec.sas;"'
```

When using the Enterprise Guide Administrator, you specify this -INITSTMT option on the server setup screens by typing the following text in the SAS Server Startup Statements box on the Options tab:

```
%INCLUDE "/home/user/autoexec.sas";
```

As an alternative, you can add the -INITSTMT option to the -sasCommand option in the SAS Object Spawner configuration file.

Why Do Platform-Specific System Commands Fail?

The starting parameters for the SAS Object Spawners that start the SAS server sessions can have an impact on the permitted functionality of the SAS code submitted to run on the server. Statements such as X, %SYSEXEC, SYSTASK, and CALL SYSTEM; the SYSTEM function; and the FILENAME option PIPE will not work unless the -ALLOWXCMD or -NONOXCMD parameter is explicitly added to the Object Spawner configuration. However, the use of these options should only be permitted with great caution, because other platform-specific operating system commands can also be submitted from submitted SAS code, which could be dangerous when used by inexperienced or malicious users!

If you are running a SAS version before 9.4, even if you only run your SAS code on the local server, you will not be able to use statements such as X, %SYSEXEC, SYSTASK, and CALL SYSTEM; the SYSTEM function; and the FILENAME option PIPE unless you have allowed operating system commands. The local server parameters are stored in the Windows Registry and can be changed as follows (only after you make a backup of the Windows Registry, because any manual updates of the Registry can impact the operation of Windows!):

1. Choose Start ➤ All Programs ➤ Accessories ➤ System Tools ➤ Backup.

2. Select Back Up Files And Settings, and then click Next.

3. Select Let Me Choose What To Back Up, and then click Next.

4. Expand My Computer, select System State, and then click Next.

5. Click Browse to select a location for the backup, click Save, click Next, and then click Finish to start the backup.

6. To edit the Windows Registry, choose Start ➤ Run, type REGEDIT, and click OK.

7. Select HKEY_CLASSES_ROOT with CLSID=440196D4, and click the LocalServer32 key.

8. Right-click Default, and choose Modify.

9. Remove -noxcmd, which should be the last item in the list, and click OK.

10. Choose View ➤ Refresh.

11. Exit the Registry window.

Changing the Current Directory

When you start a server SAS session, the current directory is always your home directory on the server platform, such as C:\WINDOWS\System32 on Windows or /home/*user* on Linux or Unix. To change this to a different location, you must have the ability to run operating system commands (see the section "Why Do Platform-Specific System Commands Fail?"). Any of the six techniques described next are applicable:

- X statement

    On a Windows server:

    ```
    OPTIONS NOXSYNC NOXWAIT;

    X 'd:; cd d:\data\lib';
    ```

    On a Linux or Unix server:

    ```
    OPTIONS NOXSYNC NOXWAIT;

    X 'cd /data/lib';
    ```

- %SYSEXEC statement

    On a Windows server:

    ```
    OPTIONS NOXSYNC NOXWAIT;

    %SYSEXEC d:;
    %SYSEXEC cd d:\data\lib;
    ```

On a Linux or Unix server:

```
%SYSEXEC cd /data/lib;
```

- SYSTASK statement

On a Windows server:

```
OPTIONS NOXSYNC NOXWAIT;

SYSTASK COMMAND 'd:; cd d:\data\lib';
```

On a Linux or Unix server:

```
OPTIONS NOXSYNC NOXWAIT;

SYSTASK COMMAND 'cd /data/lib';
```

- CALL SYSTEM statement

On a Windows server:

```
OPTIONS NOXSYNC NOXWAIT;

DATA _NULL_;
  CALL SYSTEM('d:; cd d:\data\lib');
RUN;
```

On a Linux or Unix server:

```
OPTIONS NOXSYNC NOXWAIT;
DATA _NULL_;
  CALL SYSTEM('cd /data/lib');
RUN;
```

- SYSTEM function

On a Windows server:

```
OPTIONS NOXSYNC NOXWAIT;

DATA _NULL_;
  rc = SYSTEM('d:; cd d:\data\lib');
RUN;
```

On a Linux or Unix server:

```
OPTIONS NOXSYNC NOXWAIT;

DATA _NULL_;
  rc = SYSTEM('cd /data/lib');
RUN;
```

- FILENAME statement with the PIPE option

On a Windows server:

```
FILENAME cmd PIPE 'd:; cd d:\data\lib';

DATA _NULL_;
  INFILE cmd TRUNCOVER;
  INPUT;
  PUT _INFILE_;
RUN;
```

On a Linux or Unix server:

```
FILENAME cmd PIPE 'cd /data/lib';

DATA _NULL_;
  INFILE cmd TRUNCOVER;
  INPUT;
  PUT _INFILE_;
RUN;
```

Generating SAS Code Using Enterprise Guide Tasks

All the GUI tasks in EG generate SAS code that can be submitted automatically, but using the Preview Code option gives you an opportunity to copy the generated code prior to submission and paste it into a separate SAS code node in EG to edit and run later, as shown in Figure 6-1.

```
Code Preview for Task                                                                                    ⊠
☐ Show custom code insertion points                                                               Clear All
 12  /* ------------------------------------------------------------------
 13      Sort data set SASHELP.BASEBALL
 14  ------------------------------------------------------------------ */
 15 ⊟PROC SORT
 16      DATA=SASHELP.BASEBALL(KEEP=nRuns Team)
 17      OUT=WORK.SORTTempTableSorted
 18      ;
 19      BY Team;
 20  RUN;
 21  TITLE;
 22  TITLE1 "Distribution analysis of: nRuns";
 23  FOOTNOTE;
 24  FOOTNOTE1 "Generated by the SAS System (&_SASSERVERNAME, &SYSSCPL) on %TRIM(%QSYSFUNC(DATE(), NLDA
 25      ODS EXCLUDE EXTREMEOBS MODES MOMENTS QUANTILES;
 26
 27      GOPTIONS htext=1 cells;
 28      SYMBOL v=SQUARE c=BLUE h=1 cells;
 29      PATTERN v=SOLID
 30      ;
 31 ⊟PROC UNIVARIATE DATA = WORK.SORTTempTableSorted
 32          CIBASIC(TYPE=TWOSIDED ALPHA=0.05)
 33          MU0=0
 34  ;
 35      BY Team;
 36      VAR nRuns;
 37      HISTOGRAM /      CFRAME=GRAY CAXES=BLACK WAXIS=1  CBARLINE=BLACK CFILL=BLUE PFILL=SOLID ;
 38
 39  /* ------------------------------------------------------------------
 40      End of task code
 41  ------------------------------------------------------------------ */
 42  RUN; QUIT;
```

Figure 6-1. *Preview code generated by the Distribution Analysis task*

Automatically Saving Logs to Disk

By default, EG stores logs in the project file, and not to disk. However, you can add an Export node to automatically save the log to disk, either to a locally referenced folder using the local server, or to a folder connected to the remote server.

To create an export node for a log, you must have already run the code and generated a log:

1.   Open the Project Explorer.

2.   Find the log you wish to export, and right-click it.

3.   Choose Export ➤ Export Log As A Step In Project.

4.   Click Next.

5.   Select Log File (*.log) in the list, and click Next.

6.   Select the SAS Servers radio button, and click Edit.

7.   Double-click the appropriate server on the list, find the correct folder, edit the filename, and then click Save.

8.   Click Next, and then

9.   Click Finish.

Saving the SAS log as a file on disk is generally used by clinical-trials programmers as proof that this program was run on a particular date. However, the benefits of EG are geared more toward improving the development environment, rather than production running of SAS programs; so, I do not advocate saving log files from within EG, but rather rerunning the finalized program using Batch SAS when all log and output files will be automatically saved.

Conclusions

Introducing EG as the preferred development environment for SAS programmers, particularly those working with clinical trials, allows companies to achieve the following objectives:

- Replacing a full PC SAS installation on the programmer's desktop with a single application (EG), which reduces time spent updating licensing each year

- Centralizing the updating of SAS software onto a single server or a small number of them

- Giving developers access to up-to-date programs and data without significant network delays, provided large files are not generated when programs run

- Using copies of the EG project files as templates for new studies with minimal amendments by using program nodes to set up the location of the folders, which are saved with the EG project file and not to disk

References

- Philip R. Holland, *Saving Time and Money Using SAS*, chapter 6 (SAS Press, 2007).

CHAPTER 7

■ ■ ■

Running SAS Programs in SAS Studio or Enterprise Guide

SAS Studio (previous known as SAS Web Editor) was introduced in SAS 9.4 M1 as an alternative programming environment to Enterprise Guide (EG) and interactive SAS (Display Manager System [DMS]). SAS Studio is different than EG and DMS in many ways. As a programmer, I currently use EG to help me code, test, maintain, and organize my SAS programs. I have interactive SAS installed on my PC, but I still prefer to write my programs in EG because I know it will save my log and output whenever I run a program—even if that program crashes and takes the SAS session with it! So should I now be using SAS Studio instead, and should you be using it too?

In the early 1980s, SAS offered users a ? to prompt them to type in programming statements. In the late 1980s, DMS was introduced, which let users view their code, log, and output together. It was not until the beginning of this century that EG was introduced and offered interactive access to remote SAS servers from a Windows PC. Finally, in 2014, SAS Studio was introduced for users on any platform that can be used to access a suitable web browser—the interface to SAS is a web page.

This chapter looks at the interactive options available for a range of users: those on Windows, Unix or Linux, or Mac; academics; non-programming data analysts; novice and intermediate programmers; power users; and interface and task developers. The discussion will help you decide whether SAS Studio is your best choice.

Platform-Specific Users

The programming environments available depend on the platform you are using. When options for particular types of users are discussed later, the environments also need to be taken into account.

Windows Users

The SAS System and EG run on the Windows platform. The addition of SAS Studio running in a web browser means all the programming environments discussed in this chapter are available to Windows PC users. This is not necessarily the case for the other platforms, though.

Display Manager System (DMS)

DMS is the standard interactive programming environment for SAS programmers who have the SAS System installed on their Windows PC. By default, there are five areas with information about the SAS programming environment, as shown in Figure 7-1:

- *Editor*: Used for viewing and editing SAS code

- *Log*: Displays progress and messages generated by running SAS programs

- *Output*: Displays the text report output generated by SAS programs

- *Explorer*: Lets you find and view folders and files, including SAS libraries, data sets, and external files

- *Results*: Lets you find and review output from SAS programs in all file formats produced by those programs

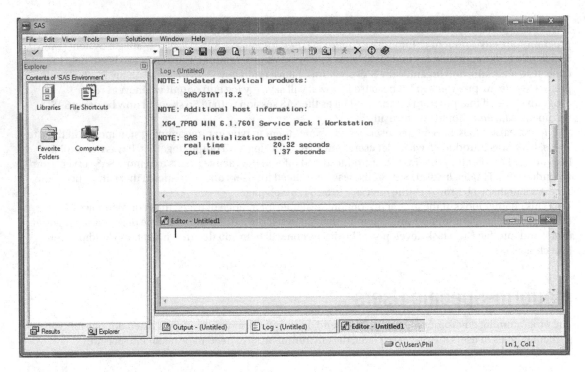

Figure 7-1. *Opening screen for interactive SAS 9.4 on a Windows PC*

Enterprise Guide

The EG view of the programming environment is much more structured and initially displays three areas of information, as shown in Figure 7-2:

- *Project Tree*: Lists the files associated with each process flow contained in the EG project. These files can be SAS programs and output files.

- *Process Flow*: Displays the files associated with a process flow in the form of a flowchart.

- *Servers*: Has five icons at the top that you can click to display the following information:

  - *Tasks*: Screens and menus that can generate SAS code

  - *SAS folders*: Data locations predefined by server administrators

  - *Servers*: SAS servers your EG session is connected to, and the files and SAS libraries accessible of those servers

  - *Prompt Manager*: Tool you can use to generate macro variable values to customize your SAS programs

  - *Data Exploration History*: Lets you easily view and subset multiple SAS data sets without them being adding automatically to the project

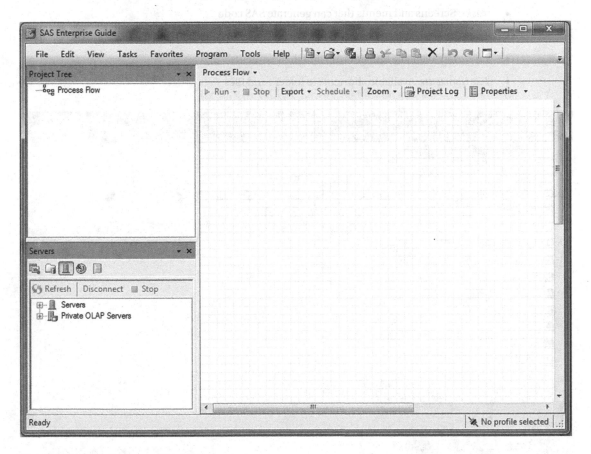

Figure 7-2. Opening screen for EG 7.1

SAS Studio

SAS Studio gives a view of the programming environment that is somewhere between those of DMS and EG. It includes four main areas of information, as shown in Figure 7-3:

- *Code*: Used to view and edit SAS code.

- *Log*: Displays the progress and messages generated by running SAS programs.

- *Results*: Displays the report output generated from SAS programs.

- The area on the left has five expanding sections:

  - *Folders*: A folder view of the connected SAS server, which could be the user's Windows PC if SAS is installed on it

  - *Tasks*: Screens and menus that can generate SAS code

  - *Snippets*: Generalized fragments of SAS code that can be pasted into the Code area

  - *Libraries*: Available SAS libraries and their contents

  - *File Shortcuts*: Available shortcuts to folders and files

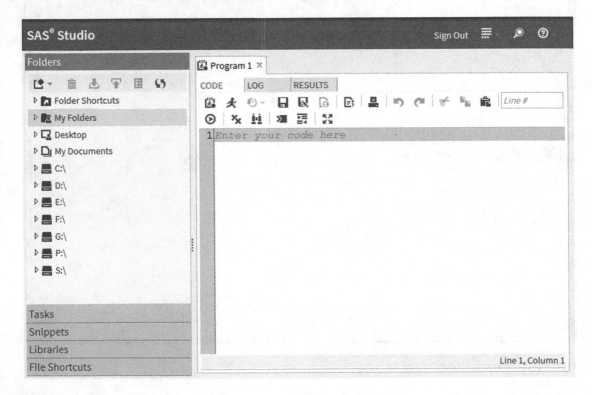

Figure 7-3. *Opening screen for SAS Studio 3.2 connected to a Windows PC*

Unix or Linux Users

The SAS System runs on most varieties of Unix and Linux. Web browsers are included in Unix and Linux installations, so users with access to these platforms have the choice of using DMS or SAS Studio to develop SAS programs.

Display Manager System (DMS)

This is the standard interactive programming environment for SAS programmers who have access to the SAS System installed on Unix or Linux. As in Windows, there are five areas with information about the SAS programming environment, but in Unix and Linux they are displayed as separate floating windows, as shown in Figure 7-4:

- *Program Editor*: Used for viewing and editing SAS code

- *Log*: Displays progress and messages generated by running SAS programs

- *Output*: Displays the text report output generated from SAS programs

- *Explorer*: Lets you find and view folders and files, including SAS libraries, data sets, and external files

- *Results*: Lets you find and review output from SAS programs in all file formats produced by SAS programs

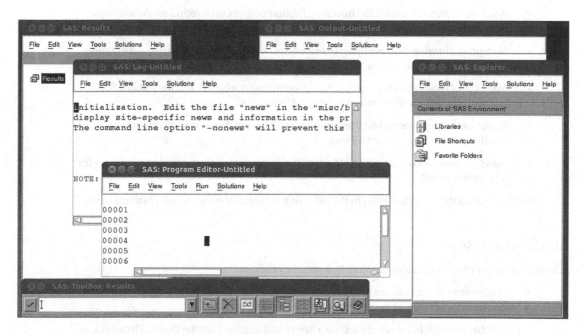

Figure 7-4. *Opening screen for interactive SAS 9.3 on Ubuntu Linux*

SAS Studio

The screen displayed by SAS Studio on a Unix or Linux platform depends completely on the type of SAS server it is connected to, but broadly speaking it looks like the screen displayed on a Windows platform. The differences are only seen in the Folders area, where a Windows server shows Windows-specific file naming with \ separators, whereas Unix and Linux servers show Unix-specific file naming with / separators.

MAC Users

The SAS System can no longer be installed on Mac computers. The only available option is to use SAS Studio in a web browser.

SAS Studio

Like the SAS Studio screen on Windows, Unix, and Linux platforms, the only differences are due to the SAS server platform, not where the web browser is being used.

Role-Specific Users

The roles in the following sections have been selected to highlight specific functionality:

- *Academic users*: Users of SAS University Edition or SAS OnDemand for Academics, both of which use SAS Studio as their interactive programming environment

- *Non-programming data analysts*: Users who access SAS data but do not necessarily need to write SAS programs

- *Novice and intermediate programmers*: Programmers who are learning about SAS but are not necessarily required to write SAS code yet

- *Power users*: Experienced SAS programmers who want to write SAS code rather than use the menus to generate SAS code

- *Interface and task developers*: XML or .NET developers who are creating new tasks for SAS Studio or EG

The options available to all the roles in the following sections depend on the platform used.

Academic Users

Academic access to SAS is available through two specific products:

- *OnDemand for Academics* uses the web-based SAS Studio interface to access a remote SAS server where course files are stored and submitted.

- *SAS University Edition* is supplied via a free virtual machine for the Oracle VirtualBox and VMware Player virtualization software packages, both of which can also be installed for free. The virtual Linux SAS 9.4 server runs on the user's 64-bit Windows, Linux, or Mac computer, but it can only be accessed through a web browser by using the IP address supplied by the running virtual machine, which starts a SAS Studio session. The web page that starts SAS Studio includes web links to discussion communities, installation documentation, and frequently asked questions, as shown in Figure 7-5.

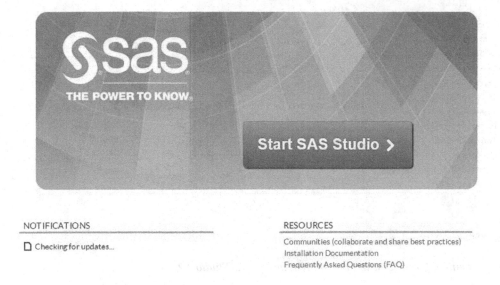

Figure 7-5. *Opening screen for SAS University Edition*

Once the SAS University Edition has been started, all the functionality of SAS Studio is available. Users may be non-programming data analysts, novice and intermediate programmers, or power users; the following sections explain the relevant features of SAS Studio.

Non-Programming Data Analysts

Because of the built-in tasks available in EG and SAS Studio, and the fact that they can generate and run SAS code without the user being aware they are doing so, non-programming data analysts can use either of these products to investigate SAS data by using menus, variable lists, and drag-and-drop operations.

SAS Studio

Let's use the Distribution Analysis as an example. You can find it in the statistics-related tasks, as shown in Figure 7-6.

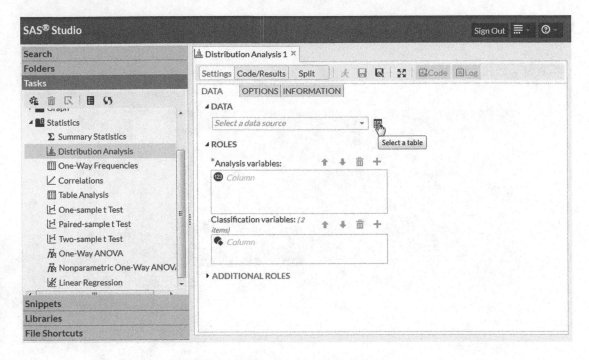

Figure 7-6. *Settings for the Distribution Analysis task in SAS Studio 3.2*

The Settings menu requires a Data option, which you can select by clicking the icon at the right end of the box; choose SASHELP.BASEBALL from the pop-up list. Select roles from the similar pop-up lists to complete the information about the data for the analysis, as shown in Figure 7-7.

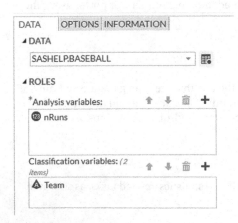

Figure 7-7. *Completed data for the Distribution Analysis task in SAS Studio*

The Options tab gives you choices about how to display the data. Then the Run icon becomes clickable, as shown in Figure 7-8.

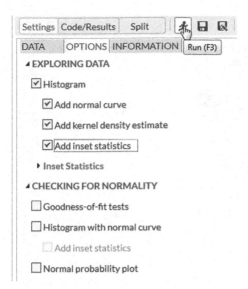

Figure 7-8. *Completed options for the Distribution Analysis task in SAS Studio*

Clicking Run starts a SAS program running. It generates the results you were looking for, as shown in Figure 7-9, without any SAS programming skills required.

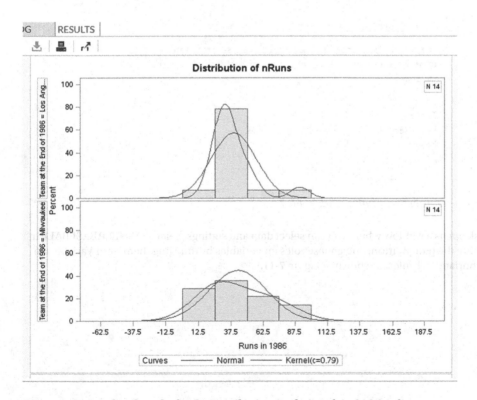

Figure 7-9. *Graphical results for the Distribution Analysis task in SAS Studio*

Enterprise Guide

Again, take the Distribution Analysis as an example. You can find it in the Tasks list in the Servers area, as shown in Figure 7-10, as well as in the Tasks list in the Servers area.

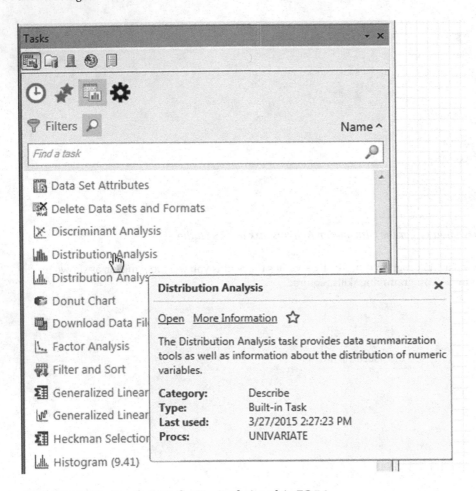

Figure 7-10. *Finding the Distribution Analysis task in EG 7.1*

Clicking the task opens a window where you can select data and settings. Select SASHELP.BASEBALL in the Data tab by clicking the [Edit] button, and choose roles for variables by dragging them from Variables to assign into the appropriate Task roles, as shown in Figure 7-11.

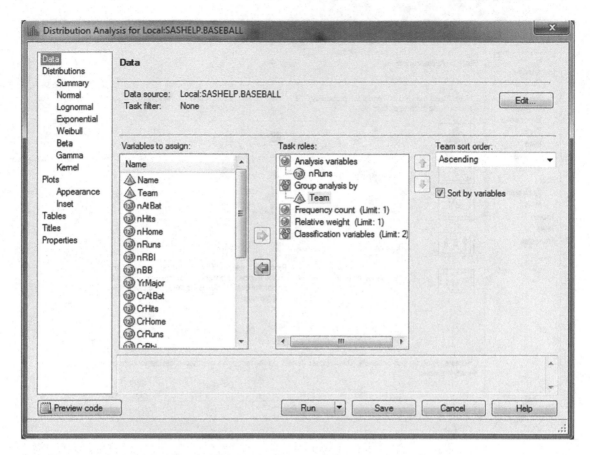

Figure 7-11. *Completed data for the Distribution Analysis task in EG 7.1*

The Appearance tab under Plots gives you choices regarding how to display the data, as shown in Figure 7-12.

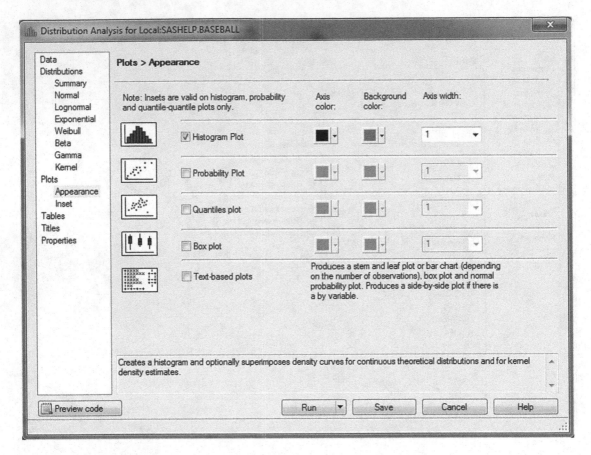

Figure 7-12. *Completed Appearance tab for the Distribution Analysis task in EG 7.1*

Clicking the Run button starts a SAS program running. It should generate the results you were looking for, as shown in Figure 7-13, again without any SAS programming skills required.

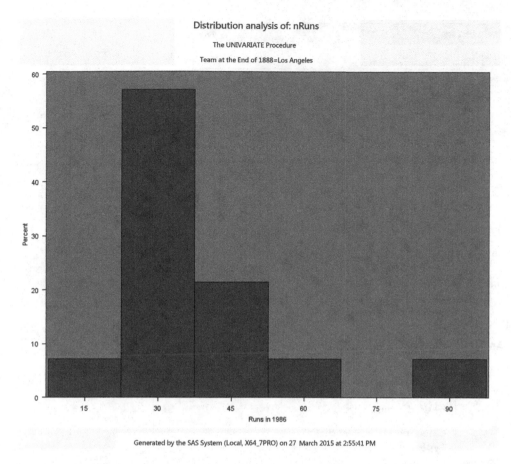

Figure 7-13. *Graphical results for the Distribution Analysis task in EG 7.1*

Enterprise Guide and SAS Studio Together

At first sight, it would appear that SAS Studio is the obvious choice, at least for Distribution Analysis, because the graphical output is much easier to view and is also easier to customize. SAS Studio uses ODS Graphics, whereas EG mostly creates traditional SAS/GRAPH plots. However, if EG and SAS Studio are installed on the same Windows PC, and a suitable web browser is also installed, EG 7.1 can use the tasks from SAS Studio, as shown in Figure 7-14: the two Distribution Analysis tasks have different icons but can only be distinguished precisely by hovering the mouse over the link. Note that you can only find both tasks in the Tasks list, because only the EG tasks are shown in the Tasks menus.

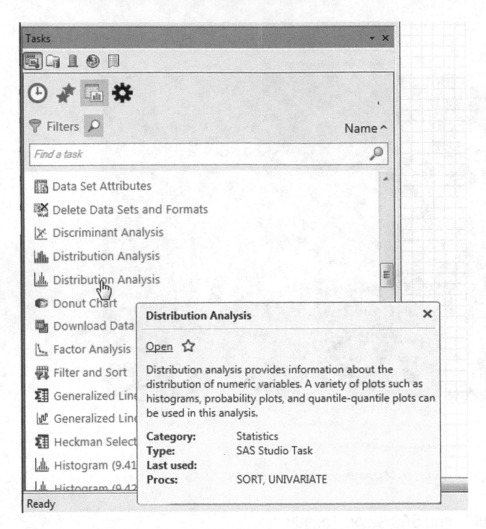

Figure 7-14. Finding the SAS Studio Distribution Analysis task in EG 7.1

Novice and Intermediate Programmers

Novice and intermediate programmers have limited SAS programming experience but wish to improve their programming skills. They also need to use SAS software to investigate data, but they do not necessarily have the SAS skills required to write code to a sufficient standard to do so unaided. Both SAS Studio and EG include functionality to give them a helping help.

SAS Studio

SAS Studio includes a small but growing list of tasks that can be used to generate SAS code to perform generic data manipulation and reporting actions. Figure 7-15 shows the data-related tasks available in SAS Studio. Each one opens a series of menus where you can specify data, report content and, appearance options.

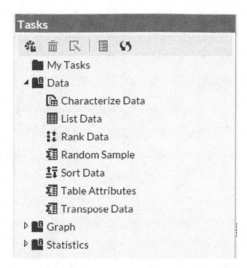

Figure 7-15. *Data-related tasks in SAS Studio 3.2*

Figure 7-16 shows the graph-related tasks available in SAS Studio. ODS Graphics code is generated for you, based on the choices made in the menus.

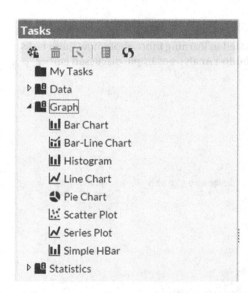

Figure 7-16. *Graph-related tasks in SAS Studio 3.2*

Figure 7-17 shows the statistics-related tasks available in SAS Studio.

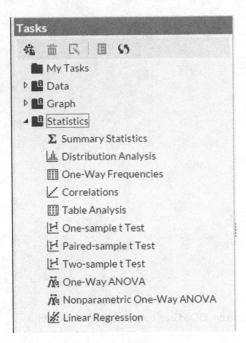

Figure 7-17. *Statistics-related tasks in SAS Studio 3.2*

As a novice or intermediate programmer, you may be interested in learning more about how these tasks work. Looking at the code generated by SAS Studio in the Distribution Analysis example discussed earlier may be helpful; see Figure 7-18.

```
14
15 ods noproctitle;
16 ods select where=(lowcase(_path_) ? 'plot' or lowcase(_path_) ? 'gram');
17
18 proc univariate data=SASHELP.BASEBALL noprint;
19     class Team;
20     histogram nRuns / normal kernel;
21     inset n / position=ne;
22 run;
```

Figure 7-18. *SAS code generated by the Distribution Analysis task in SAS Studio*

The code in Figure 7-18 is part of the generated code from a SAS Studio task. If you wish to type in some SAS code, opening a new program opens a Code tab where you can paste text that you have copied from this generated code and amend it at will. As you type code in the Code tab, useful hints and tips pop up, providing information about SAS syntax, as shown in Figure 7-19; this is another way to learn about SAS programming.

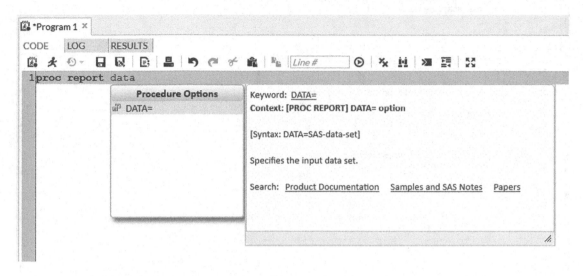

Figure 7-19. *SAS syntax hints and help in SAS Studio*

Enterprise Guide

EG includes a large and growing list of tasks you can use to generate SAS code to perform generic data-manipulation and reporting actions. As a novice or intermediate programmer, you may be interested in learning more about how these tasks work. Looking at the code generated by EG in the Distribution Analysis example discussed earlier may be helpful; see Figure 7-20.

```
Code Preview for Task                                                                      ⊠
☐ Show custom code insertion points                                              Clear All
12   /* -------------------------------------------------------------------
13       Sort data set SASHELP.BASEBALL
14       ------------------------------------------------------------- */
15 ⊟ PROC SORT
16       DATA=SASHELP.BASEBALL(KEEP=nRuns Team)
17       OUT=WORK.SORTTempTableSorted
18       ;
19       BY Team;
20   RUN;
21   TITLE;
22   TITLE1 "Distribution analysis of: nRuns";
23   FOOTNOTE;
24   FOOTNOTE1 "Generated by the SAS System (&_SASSERVERNAME, &SYSSCPL) on %TRIM(%QSYSFUNC(DATE(), NLDA
25       ODS EXCLUDE EXTREMEOBS MODES MOMENTS QUANTILES;
26
27       GOPTIONS htext=1 cells;
28       SYMBOL v=SQUARE c=BLUE h=1 cells;
29       PATTERN v=SOLID
30       ;
31 ⊟ PROC UNIVARIATE DATA = WORK.SORTTempTableSorted
32           CIBASIC(TYPE=TWOSIDED ALPHA=0.05)
33           MU0=0
34   ;
35       BY Team;
36       VAR nRuns;
37       HISTOGRAM /    CFRAME=GRAY CAXES=BLACK WAXIS=1  CBARLINE=BLACK CFILL=BLUE PFILL=SOLID ;
38
39   /* -------------------------------------------------------------------
40       End of task code
41       ------------------------------------------------------------- */
42   RUN; QUIT;
```

Figure 7-20. *SAS code generated by the Distribution Analysis task in EG 7.1*

The code in Figure 7-20 is part of the generated code from an EG task. If you wish to type in some SAS code, opening a new program opens a Code window where you can paste text that you have copied from this generated code and amend it at will. As you type code in the Code tab, useful hints and tips pop up, providing information about possible SAS keywords; see Figure 7-21.

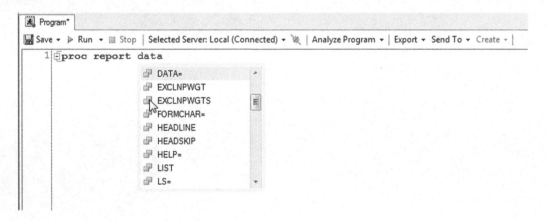

Figure 7-21. *SAS keyword assistance in EG 7.1*

Hovering the mouse over a blue keyword displays more detailed syntax help and links, as shown in Figure 7-22. This is another way to learn about SAS programming.

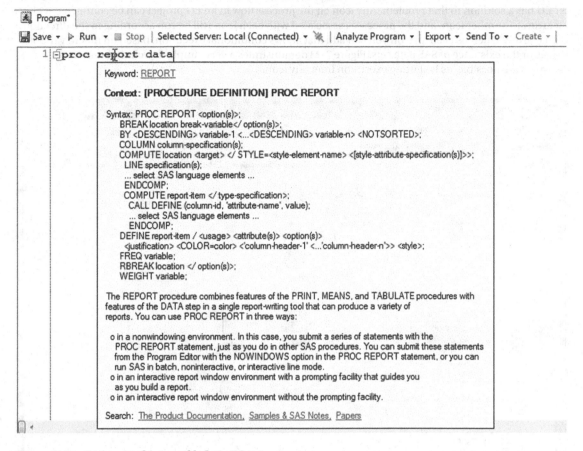

Figure 7-22. *SAS syntax hints and help in EG 7.1*

Power Users

If you are a power user, then reading to this part of the chapter has probably been an achievement in itself. Traditionally, power users have programmed everything from scratch, or, at least, started from an existing SAS program and amended it to suit their current requirements. That said, both SAS Studio and EG have features that may be of great use to power users.

Display Manager System (DMS)

Most power users are familiar with the DMS programming environment. The Enhanced Editor, Log, and Output windows are viewed as the natural way to program in SAS.

Enterprise Guide

Have you ever needed to run a collection of SAS programs in a particular order, but forgotten what that order is? EG has a solution to that problem. Any icon on the process flow in an EG project can be connected with an arrow to another icon, and the processes associated with each icon will be run according to the direction of that arrow. There is even an icon you can add that allows conditional execution, based on macro variable values or the existence of SAS data sets. Figure 7-23 demonstrates a very simple flowchart; branching networks are possible, as is starting execution from any icon.

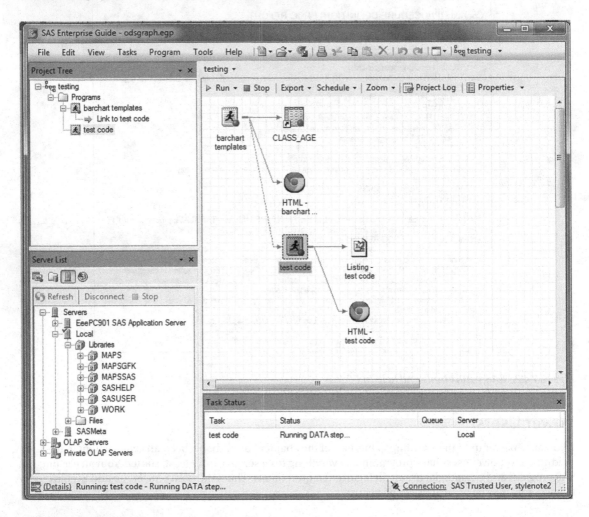

Figure 7-23. *Connected program nodes in EG 7.1*

Many other features of EG can be helpful to power users:

- Matching brackets can be highlighted, as shown in Figure 7-24. You can easily indent selected code by pressing Ctrl+I; pressing Ctrl+Z restores the previous layout if you don't like the changes. Examples of unformatted and indented code are shown in Figures 7-25 and 7-26, respectively. You can also customize how and when the indenting is done. A log summary displays a list of ERROR, WARNING, and NOTE messages from the log.

```
1 □DATA test;
2      SET sashelp.vcolumn
3           (WHERE = (UPCASE(libname) = 'SASHELP'
4                     AND UPCASE(memname) = 'CLASS'
5                     AND UPCASE(name)
6                          IN ('NAME' 'SEX' 'AGE' 'HEIGHT' 'WEIGHT') ) );
7 └ RUN;
```

Figure 7-24. *Highlighting matching brackets in EG 7.1*

```
1 □DATA test;
2  SET sashelp.vcolumn (WHERE = (UPCASE(libname) = 'SASHELP'
3  AND UPCASE(memname) = 'CLASS'
4  AND UPCASE(name) IN ('NAME' 'SEX' 'AGE' 'HEIGHT' 'WEIGHT')));
5 └ RUN;
```

Figure 7-25. *SAS code before formatting by EG 7.1*

```
1 □DATA test;
2      SET sashelp.vcolumn (WHERE = (UPCASE(libname) = 'SASHELP'
3           AND UPCASE(memname) = 'CLASS'
4           AND UPCASE(name) IN ('NAME' 'SEX' 'AGE' 'HEIGHT' 'WEIGHT')));
5 └ RUN;
```

Figure 7-26. *SAS code after formatting by EG 7.1. You can also customize how and when the indenting is done*

- The log and output are automatically retained as long as you save the EG project file.

- The program icons in the Project Tree and Process Flow views change to indicate any ERROR or WARNING messages.

- You can save links to external files on the process flow, such as PDF, DOC(X) and RTF files. Using this feature, EG project files can be project desktops, with links to all the relevant files.

SAS Studio

SAS Studio introduced the concept of *snippets* to the SAS programming environment. Basically, a snippet is a small sample of SAS code that can be pasted directly into an existing program. The snippet shown in Figure 7-27 provides some template code to import an XLS file.

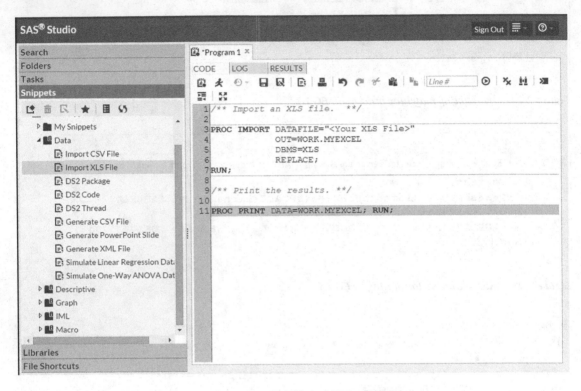

Figure 7-27. *A data-related snippet to import an XLS file in SAS Studio 3.2*

Snippets are provided for a wide range of coding situations. The snippet in Figure 7-28 provides some template code to create a horizontal bar chart using ODS Graphics.

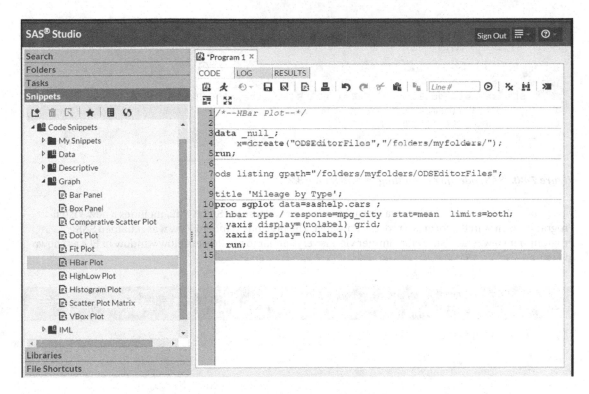

Figure 7-28. *Horizontal bar chart template code from the graph-related snippets in SAS Studio 3.2*

You may not need to be told how to import XLS files or draw horizontal bar charts in ODS Graphics, but you can also save your own snippets in My Snippets. That way, you can save SAS code that you use regularly and that is time-consuming to type, and reuse it easily in future programs.

A number of features in SAS Studio can assist power users, including formatting code.

For example, the code in Figure 7-29 becomes the code in Figure 7-30 after code formatting. However, EG is much more aware of SAS syntax, which makes its indenting of code much better than that currently in SAS Studio.

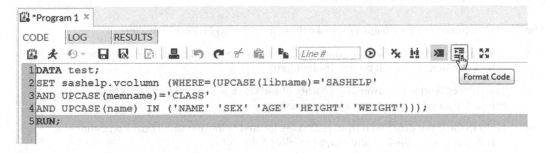

Figure 7-29. *SAS code before formatting by SAS Studio 3.2*

```
*Program 1 ×
CODE    LOG    RESULTS
1 DATA test;
2    SET sashelp.vcolumn (WHERE=(UPCASE(libname)='SASHELP' AND
3        UPCASE(memname)='CLASS' AND UPCASE(name) IN ('NAME' 'SEX' 'AGE'
4        'HEIGHT' 'WEIGHT')));
5 RUN;
```

Figure 7-30. *SAS code after formatting by SAS Studio 3.2*

Finally, SAS Studio 3.3, which was included with later releases of SAS 9.4M2, includes a new Visual Programmer view in the form of a process flow area. The previous standard view was renamed SAS Programmer view. The Visual Programmer view is very similar to the Process Flow window in EG, as shown in Figure 7-31.

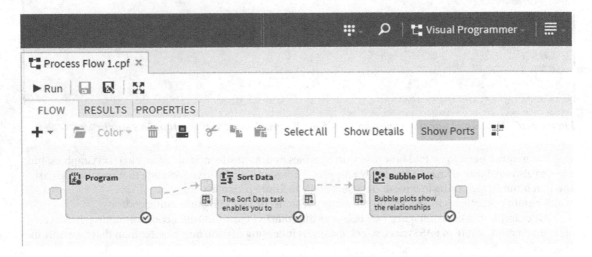

Figure 7-31. *Visual Programmer view in SAS Studio 3.3*

The Visual Programmer view's features are like those as in the EG Process Flow view:

- Items can be linked together by dragging from one of the small boxes (ports) on the side of one item to a small box on another item.

- The colored icon in the lower-right corner of each item shows whether it has been run and, if so, whether it completed successfully.

- Links to the input data and output results are located below the small boxes on either side: input data on the left, and output results on the right.

- Clicking each item opens the program or parameter view for that item.

Interface and Task Developers

The functionality of both SAS Studio and EG can be extended by writing your own custom tasks.

SAS Studio

SAS Studio tasks are based on XML files, which you can create and update in SAS Studio by clicking the New Task icon, as shown in Figure 7-32.

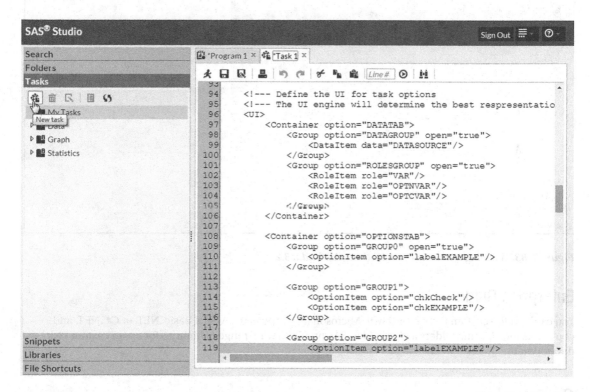

Figure 7-32. *Creating a new task in SAS Studio 3.2*

Clicking the Run (running man) icon displays the task template, as shown in Figure 7-33.

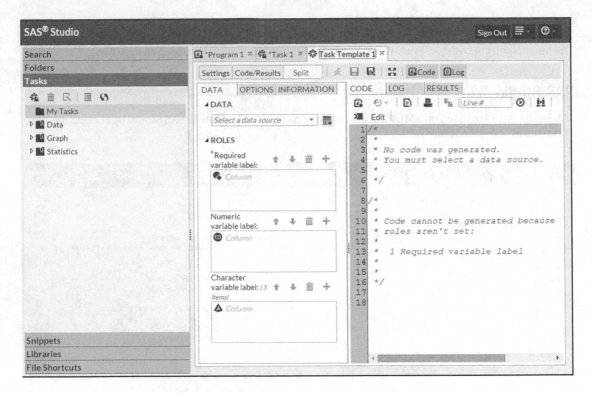

Figure 7-33. Viewing a new task template in SAS Studio 3.2

Enterprise Guide

You can develop custom tasks for EG with Microsoft .NET. You cause Visual Basic .NET, or C# .NET, and copy tasks into specific folders as `*.dll` files. SAS provide a wide range of libraries for use in custom task development.

Conclusions

This chapter asks which development environment is best for SAS programming. The answer inevitably depends on what platform you are using, but also on your SAS programming experience.

My recommendations are as follows:

- Academic users should take advantage of SAS Studio, because it is available as a free SAS programming environment in SAS University Edition.

- Novice and intermediate programmers should consider SAS Studio and Enterprise Guide as equally valid alternatives, provided they are working on Windows PCs. Otherwise, SAS Studio is the recommended option.

- Power users should, in spite of peer pressure and inertia, convert their environment of choice from DMS to EG. The change will give them access to vastly improved editing functionality, as well as the ability to create a collection of links to relevant documents.

- Interface and task developers have to consider whether they want to develop tasks for SAS Studio or EG, with the knowledge that SAS Studio tasks are also available to EG 7.1.

References

- Chris Hemedinger, *Custom Tasks for SAS Enterprise Guide Using Microsoft .NET* (SAS Press, December 2012).

CHAPTER 8

■ ■ ■

Everyday Uses for SAS Output Delivery System (ODS)

Interfacing with external programs does not necessarily require a direct connection. Sometimes, being able to create a file in the correct file format is sufficient. This chapter shows you how to prepare SAS program output suitable for Microsoft Office, OpenOffice.org/LibreOffice, Adobe Reader, or a web browser just by changing a few program statements.

The Output Delivery System (ODS) was introduced into SAS software in version 7 and replaced the various output routines used by SAS procedures, thus simplifying maintenance of the SAS reporting routines and also providing users with a standardized way to create reports. To illustrate the ODS facilities, this chapter describes a number of uses for the ODS HTML, ODS PDF, ODS RTF, ODS DOCUMENT, and ODS PACKAGE statements for reporting.

Disguising a Web Page

To be able to create Word, Excel, and PowerPoint documents from SAS programs, it is necessary to license SAS/ACCESS for PC Files. Only Base SAS is required to create HTML files (used for web pages), but there are no restrictions on what file suffix is used. Normally HTML files are saved as *.htm or *.html files, but saving them as *.xls, *.doc or *.ppt files instead will not affect the file contents. It will, however, disguise the web pages by changing the way the files are read. Office suites are often very tolerant of the internal formats of input files and will open web pages in the office application that the file extension suggests should be used (*.xls files are opened by spreadsheet applications, *.doc files are opened by word-processing applications, and so on).

Uses

This technique lets you generate formatted Microsoft Office documents directly from SAS code without having to license the SAS/ACCESS component. Each example uses the same HTML output; but by changing the file extension, you cause the program associated with that file extension to open and convert the file appropriately. Note that a warning message may inform the user about this conversion process.

Code

These examples use the functionality found in office software suites that recognizes associated applications by file extension and converts the file's contents appropriately and automatically.

ODS HTML output is read as if it were anTo make Microsoft Excel and OpenOffice.org/LibreOffice Calc read the ODS HTML output as if it were an Excel spreadsheet, you just change the file extension to ".xls":

```
ODS HTML FILE = "report.xls";
```

To make Microsoft Word and OpenOffice.org/LibreOffice Writer read the same ODS HTML output as if it were a Word document, change the file extension to ".doc":

```
ODS HTML FILE = "report.doc";
```

You can also make Microsoft PowerPoint and OpenOffice.org/LibreOffice Impress read the ODS HTML output as if it were a PowerPoint presentation by changing the file extension to ".ppt":

```
ODS HTML FILE = "report.ppt";
```

Drawbacks

The underlying data is stored in an HTML web page, so data values are displayed according to the default actions in the program reading the file (for example, numeric values with leading zeroes are reformatted in Excel and Word; the displayed precision of numeric values may be reduced in Excel; and numeric and character values in the same column are right- and left-justified, respectively, in Word).

OpenOffice.org and LibreOffice programs can read all versions of HTML. However, because Microsoft Office programs only display HTML 3 files correctly, and the default HTML produced by SAS 9 is HTML 4, you need to replace ODS HTML with ODS HTML3 to retain specified fonts and colors.

Creating Reports in Parallel

A very useful feature of ODS destinations is the ability to create many output files simultaneously. The SAS procedure described in this section internally produces a standard output that you can convert via ODS destinations to a range of different file formats.

Uses

You can generate multiple reports containing overlapping tables using a single SAS program. It is also possible to create different reports using the same ODS destination by adding an index to each ODS statement, where the index can be either a positive integer (as shown in the example code) or a character string suitable for a SAS name (that is, beginning with a letter or an underscore, followed by letters, underscores, or numbers).

Code

You can generate reports containing the same or overlapping parts of an overall report using indexed ODS statements:

```
ODS HTML(1) FILE = "report1.xls";
ODS RTF FILE = "report1.rtf";

PROC REPORT DATA = summary NOWD;
  .......
RUN;

ODS HTML(2) FILE = "report2.doc";
ODS HTML(3) FILE = "report3.xls";
ODS PDF FILE = "report4.pdf";

PROC REPORT DATA = details NOWD;
  .......
RUN;

ODS PDF CLOSE;
ODS HTML(3) CLOSE;

PROC REPORT DATA = exceptions NOWD;
  .......
RUN;

ODS HTML(2) CLOSE;
ODS RTF CLOSE;
ODS HTML(1) CLOSE;
```

The summary, details, and exceptions reports appear in `report1.xls` and `report1.rtf`, the details and exceptions reports appear in `report2.doc`, and the details report appears in `report3.xls` and `report4.pdf`.

Drawbacks

Reports can only contain information from adjacent SAS steps. Trying to append a report to an existing one by reusing a file name results in the second report overwriting the first. Note that concatenation of RTF, Word, Excel, PowerPoint, and PDF files is not possible without considerable manipulation of the file contents. You can concatenate HTML files if you include the top and bottom matter in the first and last files, respectively, but only *after* the files have been created using ODS HTML.

Saving Reports for Later

Sometimes you must reproduce part of an existing collection of reports. Because of the processing time required or the need to reproduce reports created from archived data, it may be impractical to rerun the reports. However, if you save the reports in a SAS item store using ODS DOCUMENT, then it is possible, and much quicker, to send the original reports directly to the new ODS destination from there.

Uses

All the reports generated by a program run can be stored, prior to printing, in a single file. You can then use this file to generate reports selectively to one or more destinations in a user-defined order without the need to rerun the original data processing. SAS item-store files have the "sas7bitm" extension in Windows Explorer and UNIX Unix File Manager.

Code

The example code shows how to save reports into a SAS item store using ODS DOCUMENT, how to copy a SAS item store, and how to output and manipulate reports in a SAS item store using PROC DOCUMENT:

This code saves your reports to a SAS item store:

```
ODS DOCUMENT NAME = work.doc1;

PROC MEANS DATA = sashelp.class;
  CLASS age;
  VAR height weight;
RUN;

PROC TABULATE DATA = sashelp.class;
  CLASS age;
  VAR height weight;
  TABLE (age ALL)
       ,(height*MEAN weight*MEAN);
RUN;

ODS DOCUMENT CLOSE;
```

And the following code copies the item-store file:

```
PROC COPY IN = work OUT = sasuser;
  SELECT doc1 (MEMTYPE = ITEMSTOR);
RUN;
```

Now you can produce reports from the item store without having to rerun your report processing:

```
ODS HTML FILE = "c:\temp\document.htm" STYLE = Default;

PROC DOCUMENT;
  DOC;
  DOC NAME = work.doc1;
  LIST / LEVELS = ALL;
  REPLAY;
RUN;
QUIT;

ODS HTML CLOSE;
```

You can also remove unwanted reports:

```
PROC DOCUMENT;
  DOC NAME = work.doc1;
  DELETE Means#1\Summary#1;
RUN;
QUIT;
```

Drawbacks

By default, item-store members cannot be seen in the SAS Explorer window. To allow them to be seen in SAS Explorer from SAS 9.1.3 onward, make the following changes in the Explorer options:

1. Start SAS Explorer with the EXPLORER command, or select Tools ➤ Options ➤ Explorer.

2. Select the Members tab.

3. Select ITEMSTOR in the Type list.

4. Click the Unhide button, which changes to Hide. . A Select Icon windows will appearopens:, select the ITEMSTOR icon in the Files, Folders, and Reports group, and click the OK button.

5. Click OK.

Packaging Reports into Zip Files

Introduced in SAS 9.2, the ODS PACKAGE statement lets you use ODS destinations with the SAS Publishing Framework, which is part of SAS Integration Technologies. This example, however, creates a zip file containing ODS reports without requiring the SAS Publishing Framework, so you don't need to license SAS Integration Technologies.

Uses

Creating reports containing multiple outputs can result in files that are too large to e-mail or that contain too many individual files to transmit together. Normally, a manual step is required, to copy the individual outputs into a zip file. The ability to carry out this step in SAS lets you automate and document the process without manual intervention.

The following code packages HTML and PDF outputs, together with all the files generated and required by the HTML package_frame.html file. You can also use the PROC DOCUMENT code from the previous example, instead of the PROC PRING and PROC SGPLOT code, to copy specific stored documents into the zip file.

Code

You sort the data first, because the PROC PRING output will be reported in sections by AGE:

```
PROC SORT DATA = sashelp.class OUT = temp;
  BY age;
RUN;
```

You open ODS PACKAGE using the NOPF option, which tells SAS that the SAS Publishing Framework is not required:

```
ODS PACKAGE OPEN NOPF;
```

The ODS destinations are opened in the usual way, but adding the PACKAGE option to each ODS statement tells SAS to include each ODS report in the package file:

```
ODS HTML PATH = '.' (URL = NONE) FILE = "package_body.html"
        CONTENTS = "package_contents.html" FRAME = "package_frame.html" PACKAGE;
ODS PDF FILE = "package_body.pdf" PACKAGE;

PROC PRINT DATA = temp;
  BY age;
RUN;

PROC SGPLOT DATA = temp;
  SCATTER X = age Y = height / GROUP = sex NAME = 'scatter';
  KEYLEGEND 'scatter';
RUN;

ODS HTML CLOSE;
ODS PDF CLOSE;
```

The ODS PACKAGE PUBLISH statement specifies the package type (ARCHIVE) and the name and path of the package file. The ODS PACKAGE CLOSE statement uses the CLEAR option to tell SAS to remove all the files after they have been copied into the package file, so that no temporary files are left behind:

```
ODS PACKAGE PUBLISH ARCHIVE
            PROPERTIES(ARCHIVE_NAME = "package_html_pdf_output.zip" ARCHIVE_PATH = ".");
ODS PACKAGE CLOSE CLEAR;
```

Drawbacks

Currently the ODS EXCEL destination does not include PACKAGE in its statement options in SAS 9.4M2, so Excel 2010 files cannot yet be included in zip files. Another potential drawback for companies that need to send password-protected zip files is that, currently, ODS PACKAGE does not include functionality to add passwords to the zipped items.

Conclusions

Simplifying the interface to output external files has allowed SAS to quickly expand the number of ODS destinations available to SAS users, without having to update any of the SAS procedures. The current list of available ODS destinations built into SAS 9.4M2 is as follows:

- CSVALL: Comma-separated values text file

- DOCUMENT: ODS document

- EPUB, EPUB3: ePub format for e-book readers

- EXCEL: Microsoft Excel 2010 format (*.xlsx)

- HTML, HTML3, HTML4, HTML5, CHTML, PHTML: Web page

- LISTING: Plain text file

- MARKUP: Markup language tagsets

- OUTPUT: SAS data set

- PDF: Portable Document Format (Adobe)

- POWERPOINT: Microsoft PowerPoint 2010 format (*.pptx)

- PRINTER, PCL, PS: Printable output

- RTF: Rich Text Format

PART III

■ ■ ■

Data Visualization

Overview

My interest in creating graphs with SAS goes back to the early versions of SAS/GRAPH in SAS 82.4, when I produced plots with mainframe SAS on screen or using pen plotters. In 2006, preproduction ODS Graphics was introduced in SAS 9.1.3, allowing types of graphs that were previously practical only in R to be created in SAS. This part of the book explains how to use ODS Graphics to generate high-quality graphs:

- Chapter 9, "Introduction to Graph Templates and ODS Graphics Procedures," introduces graph templates and ODS Graphics procedures, and shows how to create your own graph templates.

- Chapter 10, "Generating Graph Templates," walks you through the functionality of the ODS Graphics Designer. You learn to interactively create graph templates from two different starting points, after which the chapter explains how to generate graphs from graph templates using a DATA _NULL_ step and PROC SGRENDER.

- Chapter 11, "Converting SAS/GRAPH Plots to ODS Graphics," explains how to re-create simple SAS/GRAPH plots using ODS Graphics.

- Chapter 12, "Converting SAS/GRAPH Annotate to ODS Graphics," explains how to re-create simple SAS/GRAPH plots customized with Annotate using ODS Graphics.

- Chapter 13, "Customizing Graph Templates," explains the syntax of graph templates and how to customize graph templates similar to those generated in Chapters 9 and 10.

- Chapter 14, "ODS GRAPHICS Statement," discusses the syntax of the ODS GRAPHICS statement, as well as the image file formats and SAS code to create EMF image files available in different versions of SAS.

CHAPTER 9

■ ■ ■

Introduction to Graph Templates and ODS Graphics Procedures

You will see a number of new terms mentioned throughout this section of the book. STATGRAPH is the name of the template definition used for a graph template in PROC TEMPLATE, in the same way STYLE and TABLE are the definitions used for style and table templates. Graph template Language (GTL) is a subset of the PROC TEMPLATE statements designed specifically with graphics in mind; it is similar to other template subsets but has some unique features.

Graph templates are very different than traditional SAS/GRAPH programs, because they need to be displayed by rendering (that is, creating an image from data) with another SAS program step (for example, a DATA step or PROC SGRENDER). At this point it is probably best to think of graph templates as similar to macros with parameters.

You may have used a graph template before now and not realized it, because many SAS/STAT procedures can generate graphs if you add ODS GRAPHICS statements around them. PROC REG can generate a diagnostic panel of graphs, among other output, to display the results of the regression model with very little additional SAS code, as shown in the following code and in Figure 9-1:

```
ODS GRAPHICS ON;
PROC REG DATA = sashelp.class;
    MODEL height = age;
RUN;
ODS GRAPHICS OFF;
```

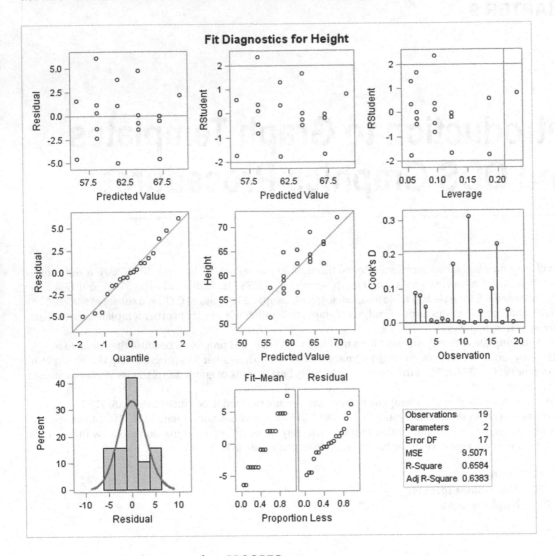

Figure 9-1. ODS Graphics output from PROC REG

Note that templates written in SAS 9.1.3 are not compatible with SAS 9.2 and beyond.

Coming Up

The rest of this part of the book takes you on a journey from easy graph-template creation using the ODS Graphics Designer to advanced techniques for updating generated templates to create flexible and reusable templates in chapter 13.

Over the years, I have standardized the way I write SAS code so that I can tell at a glance whether the text shows standard SAS text or I have supplied it. The majority of the book's code samples use the following conventions. Where the code appears not to follow these conventions, the programs were generated by SAS software, not me:

- Uppercase text is standard SAS text (for example, `ODS GRAPHICS ON`).

- Mixed-case text is user-supplied (for example, `x = y + z`).

- User-supplied parameters in `DYNAMIC` statements begin with an underscore and are in lower- or mixed-case text (for example, `_title1`).

On this journey, you are shown some data-preparation considerations, how to render data sets using graph templates, and how you can use Statistical Graphics (SG) procedures to generate templates.

Because writing graph templates manually is not a task that is recommended unless you have a lot of experience generating them, you will not see any generated-template programs until the SG procedures are introduced. The template structure and syntax are not shown until the final advanced user chapter 13.

You will learn how to develop the templates that generate the graphs shown in Figure 9-2 and Figure 9-3.

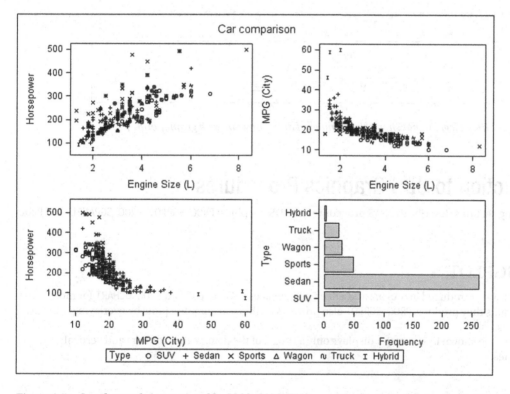

Figure 9-2. *Graph template generated by* PROC SGSCATTER, *modified to include a horizontal bar chart*

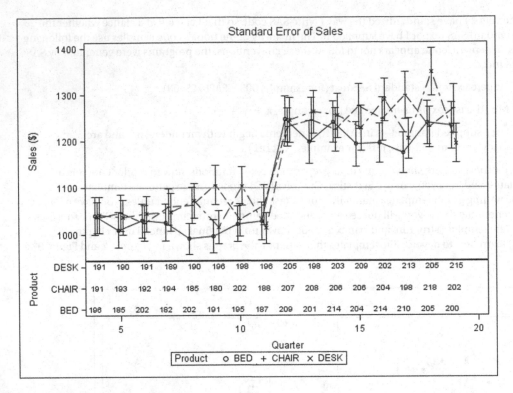

Figure 9-3. *Adding a legend that shows the number of data points in each graph point*

Introduction to ODS Graphics Procedures

The following sections describe the SAS procedures in ODS Graphics: PROC SGPLOT, PROC SGPANEL, and PROC SGSCATTER.

PROC SGPLOT

PROC SGPLOT was introduced in SAS 9.2 and effectively replaces PROC GPLOT and PROC GCHART for most of the standard graphs they produce. PROC SGPLOT also provides facilities to combine plots by overlaying them on the same axes.

The example shown in Figure 9-4 displays only a subset of the data, with error bars and vertical reference lines.

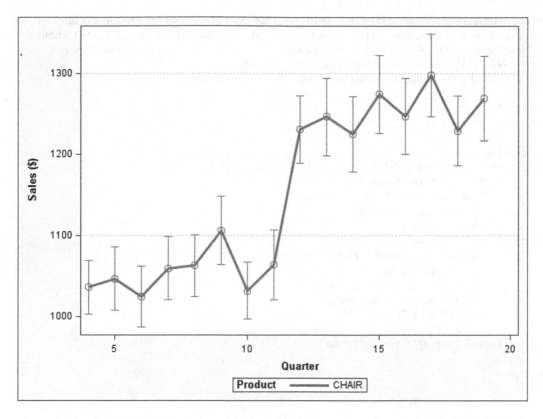

Figure 9-4. *A simple plot of connected points, error bars, and reference lines, plotted by PROC SGPLOT*

The following code was used to generate the graph. Note that a SAS program containing PROC TEMPLATE code to re-create the graph is saved to sgplot_template.sas using the TMPLOUT= option:

```
PROC SGPLOT DATA = plotdata_ods
                    (WHERE = (product = 'CHAIR'))
            TMPLOUT = "sgplot_template.sas";
  SERIES X = visitnum Y = value1 /
         MARKERATTRS = (SIZE = 10PX)
         LINEATTRS = (THICKNESS = 3PX)
         GROUP = product;
  SCATTER X = visitnum Y = value1 /
          YERRORUPPER = value1_upper
          YERRORLOWER = value1_lower
          MARKERATTRS = (SIZE = 10PX)
          GROUP = product;
  REFLINE 1100 / AXIS = Y LINEATTRS = (PATTERN = DOT);
  REFLINE 1300 / AXIS = Y LINEATTRS = (PATTERN = DOT);
RUN;
```

By comparing the graphs created by PROC GPLOT and PROC SGPLOT, you can see a number of obvious differences in their default behavior. In particular, the y-axis labels are rotated and the tick marks on both axes are sensibly spaced in PROC SGPLOT, as they are with the other SG procedures. Both features are available in PROC GPLOT but require additional parameters to achieve.

The generated graph template created by this PROC SGPLOT example is as follows:

```
proc template;
define statgraph sgplot;
begingraph;
layout overlay;
    SeriesPlot X='visitnum'n Y='value1'n / Group='PRODUCT'n
               Markerattrs=( Size=10px)
               Lineattrs=( Thickness=3px)
               LegendLabel="Sales ($)"
               NAME="series";
    ScatterPlot X='visitnum'n Y='value1'n /
               primary=true Group='PRODUCT'n
               Markerattrs=( Size=10px)
               YErrorUpper='value1_upper'n
               YErrorLower='value1_lower'n
               LegendLabel="Sales ($)"
               NAME="SCATTER";
    DiscreteLegend "series"/ title="Product";
endlayout;
endgraph;
end;
run;
```

PROC SGPANEL

PROC SGPANEL was introduced in SAS 9.2 and makes the production of multiple graphs in a grid very straightforward. It includes the majority of the features in PROC SGPLOT but also includes the PANELBY statement that specifies how the data for each panel is selected. Single or multiple panels can be generated per page, and multiple graph pages are created if the number of panels exceeds the number available on each page. Single panels (1 × 1 grids) are functionally similar to using a BY statement with PROC SGPLOT, except that the panel variable values are presented in a box above each cell.

The example shown in Figure 9-5 displays only the three sub-graphs in the available spaces in a 2 × 2 grid. But it can also be used to create a grid of graphs where the rows are based on one category value and the columns are based on another category value, allowing direct comparison of four different category value combinations in a single image.

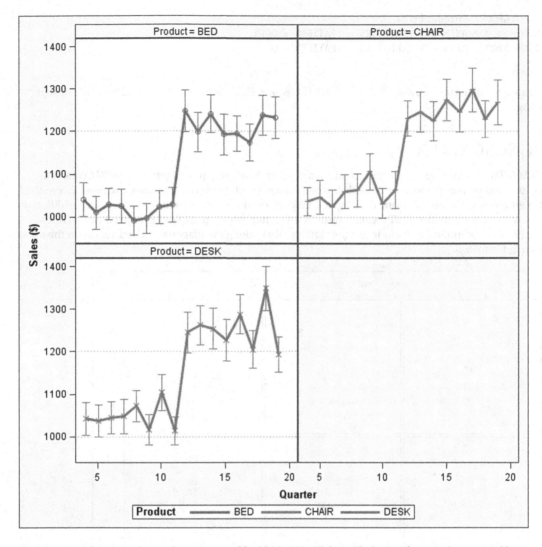

Figure 9-5. *The same plot as that generated by* PROC SGPLOT, *but split by* Product *and generated by* PROC SGPANEL

The following code was used to generate the graph in Figure 9-5. Note that no SAS program containing PROC TEMPLATE code to re-create the graph can be generated from PROC SGPANEL in SAS 9.3, because the TMPLOUT= option is no longer available:

```
PROC SGPANEL DATA=plotdata_ods;
  PANELBY product / LAYOUT = PANEL;
  SERIES X = visitnum Y = value1 /
         MARKERATTRS = (SIZE = 10PX)
         LINEATTRS = (THICKNESS = 3PX PATTERN = SOLID)
         GROUP = product;
  SCATTER X = visitnum Y = value1 /
         YERRORUPPER = value1_upper YERRORLOWER = value1_lower
         MARKERATTRS = (SIZE = 10PX)
```

```
            GROUP = product;
  REFLINE 1000 / AXIS = Y LINEATTRS = (PATTERN = DOT);
  REFLINE 1200 / AXIS = Y LINEATTRS = (PATTERN = DOT);
RUN;
```

Creating similar graphs using PROC GPLOT would require PROC GREPLAY and careful template design and sizing.

PROC SGSCATTER

PROC SGSCATTER was introduced in SAS 9.2 and has a number of different plot statements. MATRIX creates an N × N grid of sub-graphs, where each variable is plotted against each of the other variables, with either variable labels or graphs of each variable along the diagonal. COMPARE creates a row or column of sub-graphs of different variables with a common axis. PLOT creates one or more scatter sub-graphs of pairs of specified variables.

The MATRIX statement can include just the variable labels along the diagonal and tick marks on the axes, as shown in Figure 9-6.

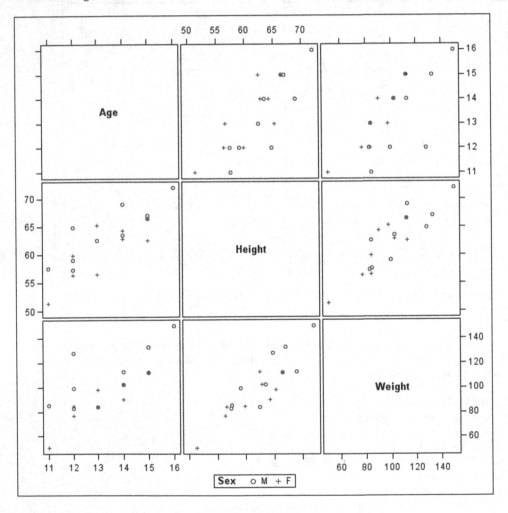

Figure 9-6. A MATRIX plot generated by PROC SGSCATTER

118

The following code was used to generate the graph in Figure 9-6. Note that a SAS program containing PROC TEMPLATE code to re-create the graph is saved to sgscatter_matrix_template1.sas using the TMPLOUT= option:

```
PROC SGSCATTER DATA = sashelp.class
               TMPLOUT = "sgscatter_matrix_template1.sas";
  MATRIX age height weight / GROUP = sex;
RUN;
```

The generated graph template created by this PROC SGSCATTER example is as follows:

```
proc template;
define statgraph sgscatter;
begingraph / designwidth=640 designheight=640;
layout gridded;
   layout lattice;
       ScatterPlotMatrix Age Height Weight / NAME="MATRIX" Group=Sex;
   endlayout;
   DiscreteLegend "MATRIX" / order=rowmajor title="Sex";
endlayout;
endgraph;
end;
run;
```

The MATRIX statement can also include any combination of histograms, normal-density curves, and kernel-density estimates of each variable along the diagonal by using the DIAGONAL= option, but this option removes the tick marks from the axes. The graph in Figure 9-7 shows only the histograms.

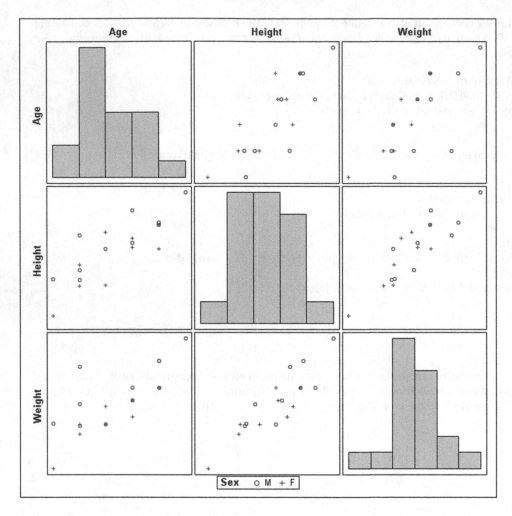

Figure 9-7. *A MATRIX plot with a DIAGONAL histogram generated by PROC SGSCATTER*

The following code was used to generate the graph in Figure 9-7, with the PROC TEMPLATE code saved to sgscatter_matrix_template2.sas using the TMPLOUT= option:

```
PROC SGSCATTER DATA = sashelp.class
            TMPLOUT = "sgscatter_matrix_template2.sas";
  MATRIX age height weight / GROUP = sex DIAGONAL = (HISTOGRAM);
RUN;
```

The generated graph template is as follows:

```
proc template;
define statgraph sgscatter;
begingraph / designwidth=640 designheight=640;
layout gridded;
   layout lattice;
```

```
        ScatterPlotMatrix Age Height Weight /
                          NAME="MATRIX" Group=Sex
                          diagonal=( histogram );
      endlayout;
      DiscreteLegend "MATRIX" / order=rowmajor title="Sex";
  endlayout;
  endgraph;
  end;
  run;
```

The graph in Figure 9-8 shows normal-density curves and kernel-density estimates together. It could include histograms, too.

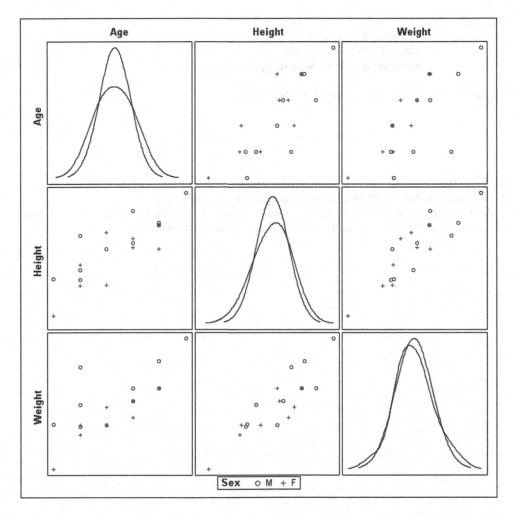

Figure 9-8. *A MATRIX plot with DIAGONAL kernel and normal plots generated by PROC SGSCATTER*

The following code was used to generate the graph in Figure 9-8, with the PROC TEMPLATE code saved to sgscatter_matrix_template3.sas using the TMPLOUT= option:

```
PROC SGSCATTER DATA = sashelp.class
               TMPLOUT = "sgscatter_matrix_template3.sas";
  MATRIX age height weight / GROUP = sex DIAGONAL = (KERNEL NORMAL);
RUN;
```

The generated graph template is given next:

```
proc template;
define statgraph sgscatter;
begingraph / designwidth=640 designheight=640;
layout gridded;
   layout lattice;
       ScatterPlotMatrix Age Height Weight /
                         NAME="MATRIX" Group=Sex
                         diagonal=( normal kernel );
   endlayout;
   DiscreteLegend "MATRIX" / order=rowmajor title="Sex";
endlayout;
endgraph;
end;
run;
```

As with PROC SGPANEL, creating graphs similar to those generated by PROC SGSCATTER but using PROC GPLOT instead would require PROC GREPLAY and careful template design and sizing.

The example shown in Figure 9-9 uses the COMPARE statement to plot a comparison of height and weight by age. The different values where sex="M" and sex="F" are shown using a Loess curve.

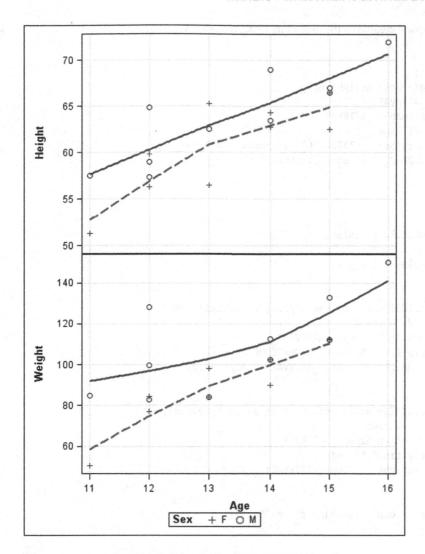

Figure 9-9. *A COMPARE plot generated by PROC SGSCATTER*

The following code was used to generate the graph:

```
PROC SGSCATTER DATA = sashelp.class
               TMPLOUT = "sgscatter_template.sas";
  COMPARE Y = (height weight) X = age /
          GROUP = sex
          MARKERATTRS = (SIZE = 10)
          LOESS = (ALPHA=0.05)
          GRID;
RUN;
```

The generated graph template created by the preceding PROC SGSCATTER example is as follows:

```
proc template;
define statgraph sgscatter;
begingraph / designwidth=480 designheight=640;
DiscreteAttrVar attrvar=__ATTRVAR1__
               var=Sex attrmap="__ATTRMAP__";
DiscreteAttrVar attrvar=__ATTRVAR1__
               var=eval(sort(Sex, RETAIN=ALL)) attrmap="__ATTRMAP__";
DiscreteAttrMap name="__ATTRMAP__" / autocycleattrs=1;
Value "M";
Value "F";
EndDiscreteAttrMap;
layout gridded;
   layout lattice / columnDataRange=union;
      ColumnAxes;
      ColumnAxis / griddisplay=on;
      EndColumnAxes;
      layout overlay /
            xaxisopts=( griddisplay=on) yaxisopts=( griddisplay=on);
         ScatterPlot X=Age Y=Height /
                     primary=true Group=__ATTRVAR1__
                     Markerattrs=( Size=10) NAME="COMPARE";
         LoessPlot X=Age Y=Height / Group=__ATTRVAR1__ Alpha=0.05;
      endlayout;
      layout overlay /
            xaxisopts=( griddisplay=on) yaxisopts=( griddisplay=on);
         ScatterPlot X=Age Y=Weight /
                     primary=true Group=__ATTRVAR1__
                     Markerattrs=( Size=10);
         LoessPlot X=Age Y=Weight / Group=__ATTRVAR1__ Alpha=0.05;
      endlayout;
   endlayout;
   DiscreteLegend "COMPARE" / order=rowmajor title="Sex";
endlayout;
endgraph;
end;
run;
```

Finally, the PLOT statement generates a grid of specified graphs, all with the same options—in this case, each with a Loess curve—as shown in Figure 9-10.

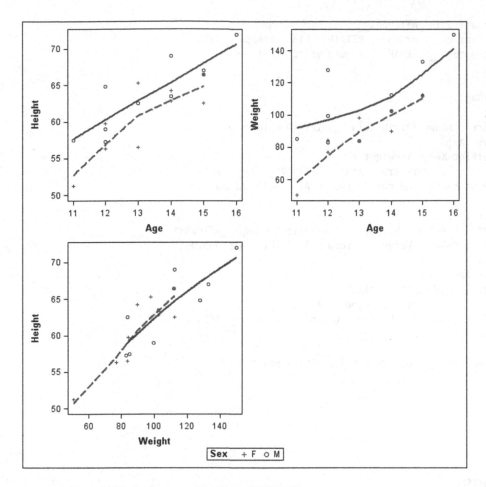

Figure 9-10. *A PLOT plot generated by* PROC SGSCATTER

The following code was used to generate this graph, with the PROC TEMPLATE code saved to sgscatter_plot_template.sas using the TMPLOUT= option:

```
PROC SGSCATTER DATA = sashelp.class
               TMPLOUT = "sgscatter_plot_template.sas";
  PLOT (height weight)*age height*weight /
      GROUP = sex LOESS = (ALPHA=0.05);
RUN;
```

The generated graph template is given next:

```
proc template;
define statgraph sgscatter;
begingraph / designwidth=640 designheight=640;
DiscreteAttrVar attrvar=__ATTRVAR1__
               var=Sex attrmap="__ATTRMAP__";
```

```
DiscreteAttrVar attrvar=__ATTRVAR1__
                var=eval(sort(Sex, RETAIN=ALL)) attrmap="__ATTRMAP__";
DiscreteAttrMap name="__ATTRMAP__" / autocycleattrs=1;
Value "M";
Value "F";
EndDiscreteAttrMap;
layout gridded;
   layout lattice / rowgutter=10 columngutter=10 columns=2;
      layout overlay;
         ScatterPlot X=Age Y=Height /
                     primary=true Group=__ATTRVAR1__ NAME="PLOT";
         LoessPlot X=Age Y=Height / Group=__ATTRVAR1__ Alpha=0.05;
      endlayout;
      layout overlay;
         ScatterPlot X=Age Y=Weight / primary=true Group=__ATTRVAR1__;
         LoessPlot X=Age Y=Weight / Group=__ATTRVAR1__ Alpha=0.05;
      endlayout;
      layout overlay;
         ScatterPlot X=Weight Y=Height /
                     primary=true Group=__ATTRVAR1__;
         LoessPlot X=Weight Y=Height / Group=__ATTRVAR1__ Alpha=0.05;
      endlayout;
   endlayout;
   DiscreteLegend "PLOT" / order=rowmajor title="Sex";
endlayout;
endgraph;
end;
run;
```

Conclusions

At this point, I hope you can appreciate that writing graph templates from scratch is definitely not an easy task. The wide range of syntax and the varied options available to the programmer make the task daunting for any beginner. It is, therefore, comforting that you can use the SGPLOT and SGSCATTER procedures to generate graph templates with much less effort and with relatively simple syntax. More methods for generating graph templates are discussed later in this part of the book, along with simple techniques to modify them so that they can be used to create a much wider range of plots.

CHAPTER 10

■ ■ ■

Generating Graph Templates

The previous chapter showed how to generate graph templates while running `PROC SGPLOT` and `PROC SGSCATTER` code. These procedures can generate graph templates on all platforms that support them (for example, Windows, Unix, Linux, and z/OS). However, these procedures are not interactive and do not allow you to see the template output directly. If you have access to an interactive SAS environment, the ODS Graphics Designer provides an interactive environment in which you can develop a graph template incrementally and see the current status of the template throughout its development.

At the end of this chapter, you see various techniques that use graph templates to render data to create graphs, and you are briefly introduced to how to prepare data for use with graph templates.

ODS Graphics Designer

The ODS Graphics Designer provides a drag-and-drop interface that lets you design a graph template while viewing the resulting graph during the development phase.

How to Start the ODS Graphics Designer

You can start the ODS Graphics Designer from within SAS 9.2 and subsequent versions with a macro call:

```
%SGDESIGN
```

It can also be started from a drop-down menu option in SAS 9.3 (see Figure 10-1), which generates this macro call.

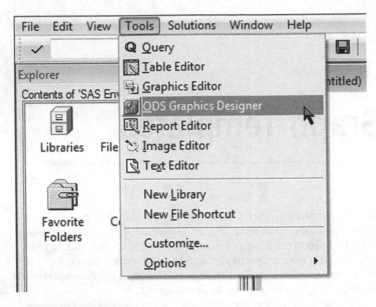

Figure 10-1. Drop-down menu

This option starts a Java application you can use to build graph templates and then send them back to SAS for execution. The screen shots in this section were taken in the SAS 9.3 version of the ODS Graphics Designer; differences between SAS 9.2 and 9.3 are noted when necessary. The screen shown in Figure 10-2 is displayed while the application is being loaded.

Figure 10-2. Splash screen for the SAS ODS Graphics Designer

Note that the ODS Graphics Designer runs on all SAS versions from SAS 9.2 M3 on Windows, Unix, and Linux platforms, but it also requires access to a correctly configured Java installation and an interactive SAS session on the same platform. An Enterprise Guide (EG) add-in for ODS Graphics Designer is available, but it has same prerequisites as EG on Windows.

The initial screen layout, shown in Figure 10-3, includes Elements and Graph Gallery sections.

The ODS Graphics Designer is not part of the SAS System, but an external program using the SAS software environment, so the SAS data sets used to create templates must be stored as permanent SAS data sets in accessible libraries. The SAS System starts with the following permanent libraries allocated by default: SASHELP, SASUSER, and MAPS.

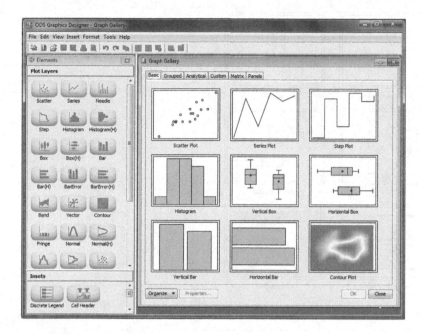

Figure 10-3. *Initial screen layout*

The following code allocates a permanent SAS library called TEST and a new SAS data set called test.cars for use with %sgdesign, prior to calling the macro:

```
LIBNAME test "C:\saslibrary\";

DATA test.cars;
  SET sashelp.ashelp cars;
  percent_saving = 100 * (msrp - invoice) / msrp;
  highway_increase = mpg_highway - mpg_city;
  cylinder_size = enginesize / cylinders;
RUN;

%SGDESIGN
```

Using the Gallery to Create Simple Templates

The Gallery, shown in Figure 10-4, provides a collection of typical graphical reports that can be used as starting points for more complex reports. They can also be used with minimal customization to generate simple templates.

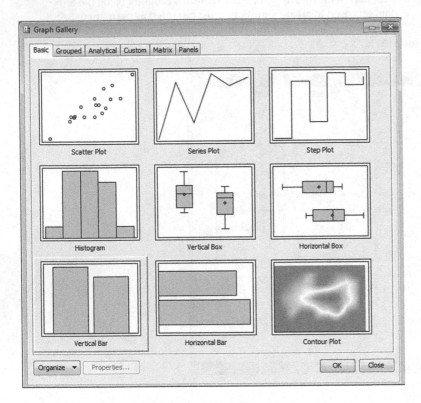

Figure 10-4. *The Gallery with Vertical Bar selected*

After you select a Gallery entry, you are asked for details of the data to be plotted, as shown in Figure 10-5. Note that in SAS 9.2, there is no Group Display option.

Figure 10-5. *Details of the data to be plotted*

You can also select the style and graph layout from a menu by right-clicking the graph (see Figure 10-6).

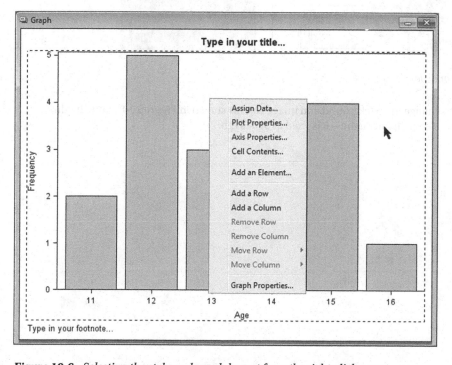

Figure 10-6. *Selecting the style and graph layout from the right-click menu*

You can use the Graph Properties option in Figure 10-6 to change the style, as shown in Figure 10-7.

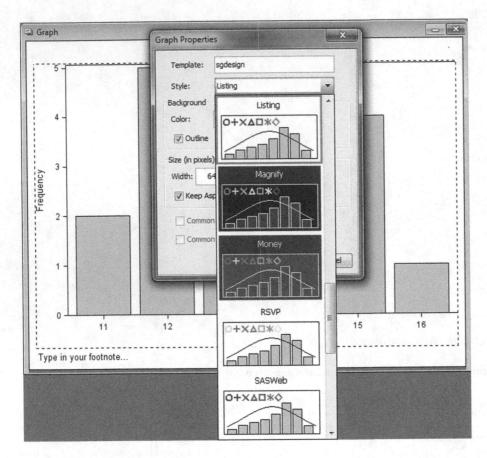

Figure 10-7. *Graph Properties option*

It is also possible to change the background and image size, as shown in Figure 10-8. Note that in SAS 9.2, you can't specify the template name—it is fixed as sgdesign.

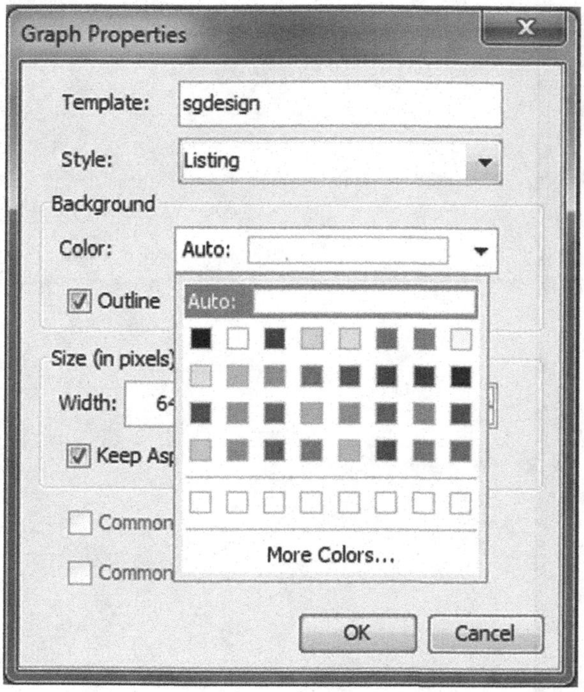

Figure 10-8. *Changing the background color*

The Plot Properties option in Figure 10-6, which is also the Plots tab on the Cell Properties window, provides a dialog in which you can change the styles used for text and other graph features, as shown in Figure 10-9.

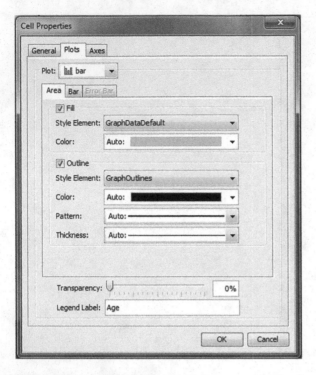

Figure 10-9. *Plot Properties option*

The Axis Properties option in Figure 10-6, which is also the Axes tab on the Cell Properties window, opens the Axes tab in the dialog opened by the Plot Properties option. You can use the Display tab to update the way each axis is displayed, as shown in Figure 10-10.

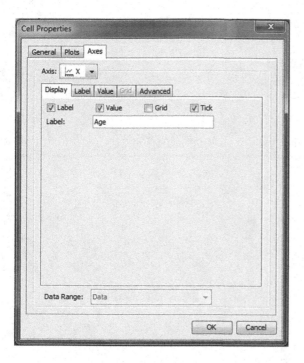

Figure 10-10. *Axis Properties dialog*

The Label tab lets you update the label style for each axis, as shown in Figure 10-11.

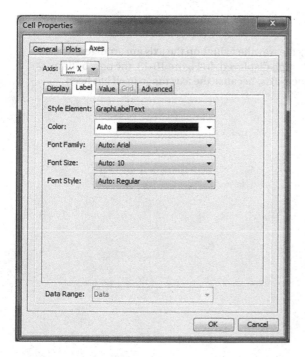

Figure 10-11. *The Label tab*

You can use the Value tab to update the value style for each axis, as shown in Figure 10-12.

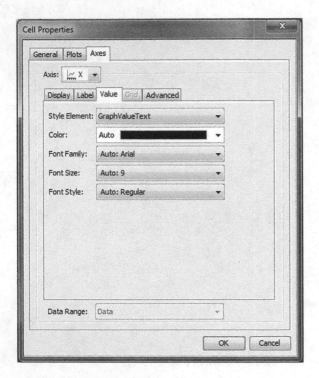

Figure 10-12. *The Value tab*

The Advanced tab gives you options for updating the way the values on the axis are arranged. These options may be grayed out, depending on the type of graph displayed. In Figure 10-13, the only option available is to reverse the order of the tick marks on the x-axis, because the axis range itself has been automated.

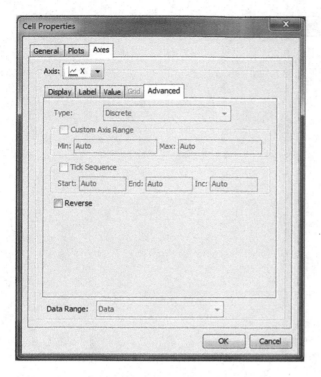

Figure 10-13. *The Advanced tab*

The Cell Contents option in Figure 10-6, which is also the General tab on the Cell Properties window, lets you update the general appearance of the graph, as shown in Figure 10-14.

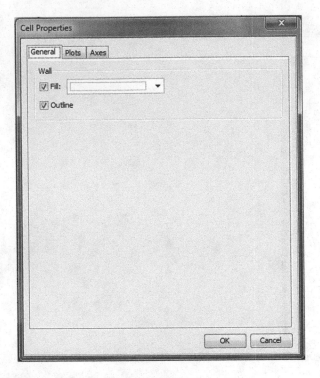

Figure 10-14. *Cell Contents dialog*

You can update the graph's titles and footnotes by double-clicking the existing text and overwriting it, as shown in Figure 10-15.

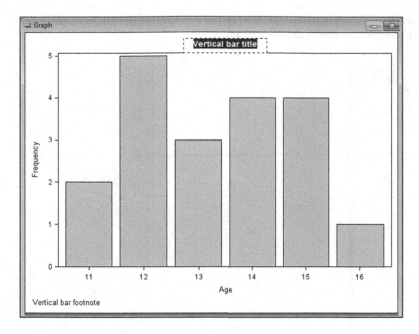

Figure 10-15. *Title and footnotes*

To view the graph and the code together (if the Code window is not already visible), choose View ➤ Code in the ODS Graphics Designer window, as shown in Figure 10-16. The template code for this graph is displayed as Template A in Graph Template Contents in Chapter 13.

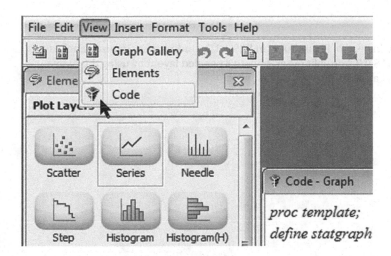

Figure 10-16. *View ➤ Code menu option*

You also have an opportunity to split the graph into a paneled layout by using the Assign Data option in Figure 10-6 and specifying Panel Variables, as shown in Figure 10-17.

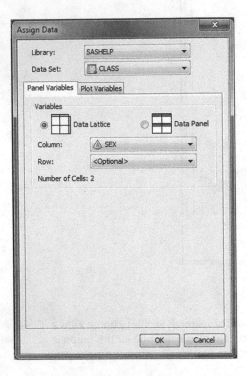

Figure 10-17. Assign Data dialog

Figure 10-18 shows what you see instead of Figure 10-17 in SAS 9.2, including a Customize Panel Layout option that is no longer available in SAS 9.3. You split the graph into a paneled layout by using the Assign Data option and specifying the Panel Variables.

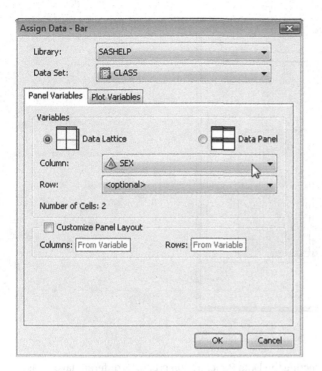

Figure 10-18. *Splitting a Graph into a paneled layout (showing the SAS 9.2 version with the Customize Panel Layout check box)*

The resulting graph shows the data split between Sex=M and F, with a gap where there is no corresponding data for Age=16 when Sex=F (see Figure 10-19). The template code for this graph is listed as Template B in Graph Template Contents in Chapter 13.

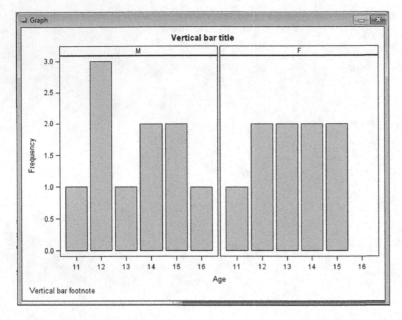

Figure 10-19. *Final graph*

Instead of arranging the data into a lattice, selecting the Data Panel option creates a different layout, as shown in Figure 10-20.

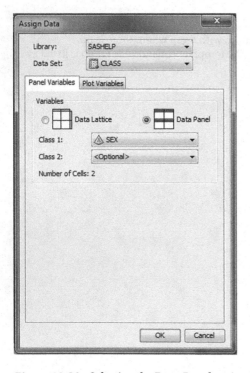

Figure 10-20. *Selecting the Data Panel option creates a different layout*

Panels are drawn with all the corresponding categorical variable values in boxes above the individual cells. Lattices are drawn with the first categorical variable value above the corresponding column of cells and the second (when used) next to the corresponding row of cells. In this case, because there are only *two* cells in the panel, the resulting graph is indistinguishable from that generated using the Data Lattice option. The template code for this graph is listed as Template C in Graph Template Contents in Chapter 13.

Building a Template from a Blank Graph

The difference between a Gallery entry and a blank graph (see Figure 10-21) is that no defaults are set, so you have much more control over the content and layout of the final template.

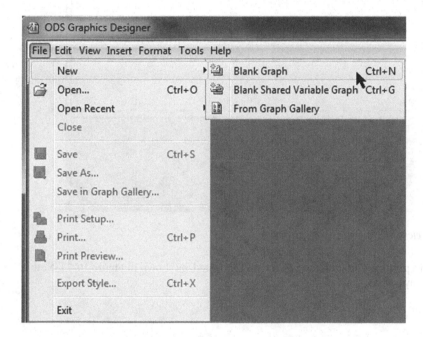

Figure 10-21. *Creating a blank graph*

A blank graph lets you add what you need. It is straightforward to add to a single graphical report multiple graphical objects that use the same data. You just drag elements from the appropriate Elements group (such as Plot Layers or Insets) onto the graph area, as shown in Figure 10-22.

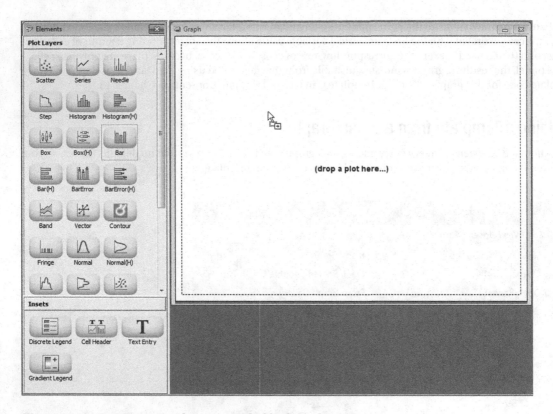

Figure 10-22. *Dragging a Bar element onto the blank graph*

Once you have dragged in a plotting element, the SAS data is requested, as shown in Figure 10-23. Note that SAS 9.2 has no Group Display option.

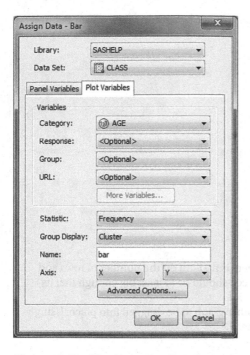

Figure 10-23. *The data to be plotted*

This approach generates a familiar graph, but without any titles or footnotes, as shown in Figure 10-24.

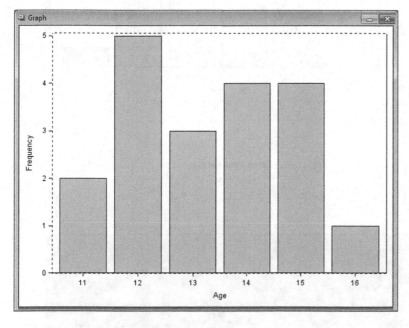

Figure 10-24. *The initially generated graph*

You can create an additional row for another graph on the same page by adding a new row under the existing graph (see Figure 10-25).

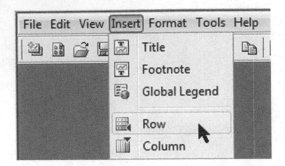

Figure 10-25. *Adding a new row from the Insert menu*

Note that you can also insert a column instead of a row. There is no limit on the number of rows and columns that can be added, other than the fact that each graph cell should be at least big enough that its contents are legible.

Figure 10-26 shows a blank row in the image, ready for another graph to be dragged into place. Using the Column menu option would have added a new column instead.

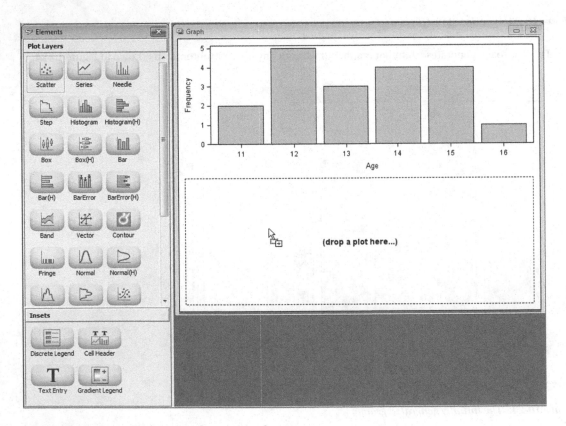

Figure 10-26. *Dragging a Scatter element into the new row*

Note that ODS Graphics Designer is only able to generate a lattice containing N1 × N2 cells, where every row contains the same number of columns and every column contains the same number of rows. A lattice that has, for example, more cells in row 1 than in row 2 requires a manual adjustment.

The data for the new graph is automatically requested, as shown in Figure 10-27. Note that the Group Display option is not included in SAS 9.2.

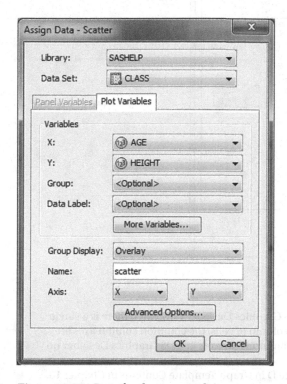

Figure 10-27. *Data for the new graph*

You can now add titles and footnotes (see Figure 10-28), but in ODS Graphics Designer they can only be *global* titles and footnotes, not specific to each cell.

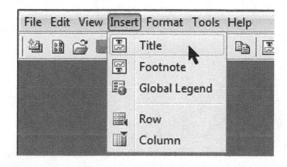

Figure 10-28. *Adding a global title from the Insert menu*

The graph is now ready for use, as shown in Figure 10-29.

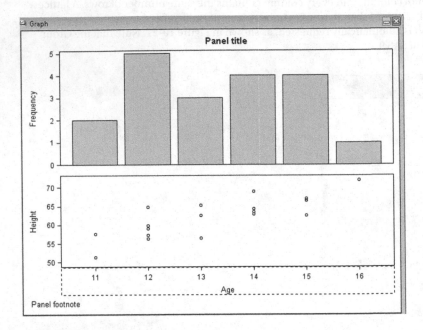

***Figure 10-29.** Final graph*

Note that common column axes are possible in ODS Graphics Designer only when there is a single column of graph cells. As soon as you add an additional column of cells, the common column axes are changed back to individual axes. However, you can use common row axes in ODS Graphics Designer no matter how many rows of cells are present.

The template code for this graph is listed as Template D in Graph Template Contents in Chapter 13.

Saving the Template as a Designer File (*.sgd)

Click the Graph window and then choose File ➤ Save As to save the template as a designer file with file type *.sgd (see Figure 10-30).

Figure 10-30. *Saving a template as a designer file*

These files can be opened and edited with ODS Graphics Designer, so you can use them to store the latest versions of the templates you are developing for later use. They can also be saved as backup copies, if you want to develop a range of templates from a single starting template. Note that these files can only be opened with ODS Graphics Designer or PROC SGDESIGN, which is not described in this book.

You can also save a template to the Gallery by clicking File ➤ Save To Gallery, which makes the template immediately available when ODS Graphics Designer is next used.

Saving the Template as a SAS Program (*.sas)

Click the Code window and then choose File ➤ Save As to save a template as a SAS program with file type *.sas, as shown in Figure 10-31.

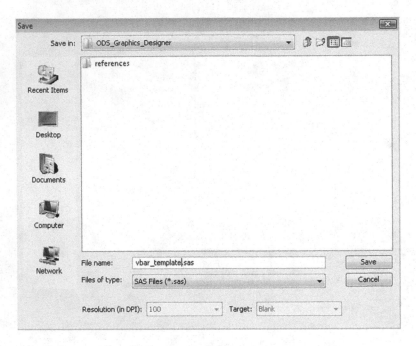

Figure 10-31. *Saving code as a SAS program*

Graph Template Usage

There are a number of steps required before a graph template can generate a graph. Firstly the data needs to be structured in a form that is suitable for the template, and then another program processes the data using the instructions stored in the graph template.

Preparing Data for Graph Templates

The following code generates simulated clinical data with visit numbers, products, and an absolute value with a standard error (for the simple line plot). The original data in sashelp.prdsal2 is very uniform, so a filter is used to make the value counts less even:

```
PROC SQL;
  CREATE TABLE plotdata AS
    SELECT INTCK('QTR', '01jan1994'd, monyr) AS visitnum
           ,product
           ,MEAN(predict) AS value1
           /*used for the simple line plots*/
           ,STDERR(predict) AS value1_se
           /*used for the simple line plots*/
           ,COUNT(*) AS count
    FROM    sashelp.prdsal2
            (WHERE = (product IN ('BED' 'CHAIR' 'DESK')
                      AND predict > 400))
```

```
    GROUP BY
          visitnum
          ,product;
QUIT;
```

The extra calculations in plotdata_ods are applied to visitnum to offset the points and prevent them from overlapping and obscuring data; to price_upper and price_lower to add upper and lower standard error points for the error bars; and to ccount to convert the numeric counts to text for the final graph to be generated from a template by PROC SGRENDER. The code looks like this:

```
DATA plotdata_ods;
  SET plotdata;
  LENGTH ccount $4;
  SELECT (product);
    WHEN ('BED') visitnum = visitnum - 0.1;
    WHEN ('DESK') visitnum = visitnum + 0.1;
    OTHERWISE;
  END;
  value1_upper = value1 + value1_se;
  value1_lower = value1 - value1_se;
  ccount = STRIP(PUT(count, 4.));
  LABEL value1 = 'Sales ($)'
        visitnum = 'Quarter';
RUN;
```

Displaying Graph Templates

You can display graph templates two ways: the DATA _NULL_ method and the PROC SGRENDER method. Generally, the PROC SGRENDER method is preferred for graph templates, unless other template types are being used at the same time; the DATA _NULL_ method is common to all template types.

DATA _NULL_

When graph templates were first introduced in SAS 9.1.3, before the introduction of PROC SGRENDER, the DATA _NULL_ step with FILE PRINT ODS and PUT _ODS_ statements was the only way to display input data using graph templates. This method is still available in SAS 9.3, but PROC SGRENDER is now preferred. The sgplot_count template is described in detail in Chapter 13. Here is an example:

```
ODS GRAPHICS ON;
DATA _NULL_;
   LENGTH ccount $4;
   SET plotdata;
   BY visitnum;
   value1_upper = value1 + value1_se;
   value1_lower = value1 - value1_se;
   ccount = STRIP(PUT(count, 4.));
   FILE PRINT ODS =
     (TEMPLATE = 'sgplot_count'
      DYNAMIC = (_title = "Figure 1. Standard Error of Sales"
                 _title2 = "Overall"
                 _footnote = "Program: &pgm..sas"
```

```
                        _xvar = "visitnum"
                        _xlabel = "Quarter"
                        _ylabel = "Bed and Chair sales ($)"
                        _yvar1 = "value1"
                        _yupper1 = "value1_upper"
                        _ylower1 = "value1_lower"
                        _nvar1 = "ccount"
                        _group = "product"
                    )
        );
    PUT _ODS_;
RUN;
ODS GRAPHICS OFF;
```

PROC SGRENDER

PROC SGRENDER was introduced in SAS 9.2. It is probably more closely related to PROC GANNO than
PROC GPLOT, because it is used to render input data using predefined graph templates. The sgplot_count
template is described in detail in Chapter 13. Here is an example:

```
PROC SGRENDER DATA = plotdata_ods
                        (WHERE = (product IN ('BED' 'CHAIR')))
            TEMPLATE = 'sgplot_count';
  DYNAMIC _title = "Sales"
          _title2 = "Bed and Chair"
          _footnote = "Program: &pgm..sas"
          _xvar = "visitnum"
          _xlabel = "Quarter"
          _ylabel = "Sales ($)"
          _yvar1 = "value1"
          _yupper1 = "value1_upper"
          _ylower1 = "value1_lower"
          _nvar1 = "ccount"
          _group = "product";
RUN;
```

Note that the highlighted ODS GRAPHICS statements required with the DATA step are no longer necessary.
They are available as options when you need to modify the size and destination of the images with any of the
Statistical Graphics (SG) procedures.

Conclusions

This chapter showed you the two main routes through ODS Graphics Designer: starting from a prepackaged
template or from a blank page. Both routes can be used to created new, prepackaged templates for later use, or
the generated PROC TEMPLATE code can be stored as a SAS program file. Once you use the PROC TEMPLATE code
to create a graph template, it can be used to render data using a DATA _NULL_ step or with PROC SGRENDER to
create an image file.

CHAPTER 11

■ ■ ■

Converting SAS/GRAPH Plots to ODS Graphics

This chapter compares the output from the most commonly used SAS code for producing plots and charts using SAS/GRAPH and ODS Graphics. Each ODS Graphics program is rated as follows:

- *Easy:* One SAS/GRAPH procedure statement can be replaced with an ODS Graphics procedure. The conversion may also require some preprocessing of the input data.

- *Difficult:* One SAS/GRAPH procedure can be replaced with code containing PROC TEMPLATE and PROC SGRENDER, or the conversion requires extensive preprocessing of the input data.

- *Impossible:* There is currently no corresponding ODS Graphics procedure in that version of SAS software to replicate the SAS/GRAPH graph.

Each plot is followed by the SAS code used to create it and is identified in the text.

Scatter Plots

The first and simplest of the commonly used plots is the *scatter plot*. Basically, many data points are scattered over the graph area.

SAS/GRAPH from SAS 9.2

Figure 11-1 shows a scatter plot from SAS/GRAPH in SAS 9.2. See Listing 11-1 for the SAS plot code.

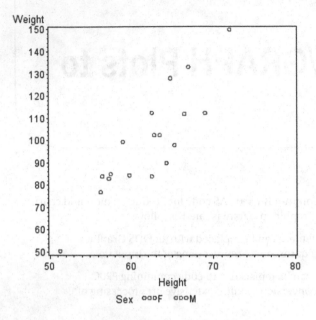

Figure 11-1. *Scatter plot created by PROC GPLOT in SAS 9.2*

Listing 11-1. PROC GPLOT Scatter Plot

```
PROC GPLOT DATA = sashelp.class;
    SYMBOL V = CIRCLE I = NONE;
    PLOT weight * height = sex;
RUN;
```

ODS Graphics from SAS 9.2 (Easy)

Note that because the input data is unsorted and the first record contains a record where sex='M', the legend begins with sex='M', as shown in Figure 11-2. See Listing 11-2 for the SAS plot code.

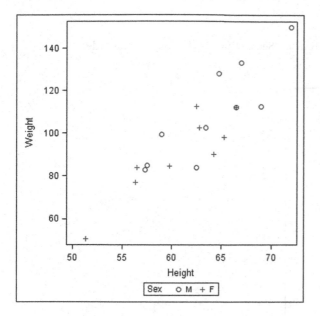

Figure 11-2. *Scatter plot created by PROC SGPLOT in SAS 9.2*

Listing 11-2. PROC SGPLOT Scatter Plot

```
PROC SGPLOT DATA = sashelp.class;
    SCATTER Y = weight X = height /
            GROUP = sex;
RUN;
```

Line Plots

The second and probably the most frequently used of the common plots is the line plot. SAS/GRAPH provides a vast range of options for how the individual points are used to create the line. The example code just joins each point to the next, which is why the points are sorted by the values on the x-axis.

SAS/GRAPH from SAS 9.2

Figure 11-3 shows a line plot from SAS/GRAPH in SAS 9.2. See Listing 11-3 for the SAS plot code.

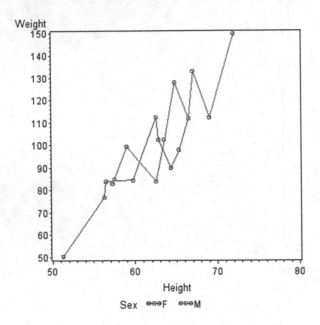

Figure 11-3. *Line plot created by PROC GPLOT in SAS 9.2*

Listing 11-3. PROC GPLOT Line Plot

```
PROC SORT DATA = sashelp.class
         OUT = class;
    BY sex height;
RUN;

PROC GPLOT DATA = class;
    SYMBOL V = CIRCLE I = JOIN;
    PLOT weight * height = sex;
RUN;
```

ODS Graphics from SAS 9.2 (Easy)

Note that the input data has been sorted, and the first record contains a record where sex='F', so the legend order matches that in the SAS/GRAPH plot. There are also fewer ticks on the two axes, as shown in Figure 11-4. See Listing 11-4 for the SAS plot code.

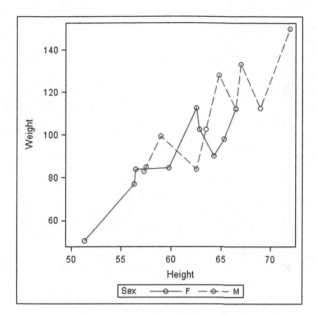

Figure 11-4. *Line plot created by PROC SGPLOT in SAS 9.2*

Listing 11-4. PROC SGPLOT Line Plot

```
PROC SORT DATA = sashelp.class
        OUT = class;
    BY sex height;
RUN;

PROC SGPLOT DATA = class;
    SERIES Y = weight X = height /
        GROUP = sex MARKERS
        MARKERATTRS = (SYMBOL=CIRCLE);
RUN;
```

Regression Plots

Another way to use points to generate a line is to calculate a regression line and confidence limits.

SAS/GRAPH from SAS 9.2

In SAS/GRAPH, the regression and confidence-limit lines are plotted well beyond the limits of the data points and extend to the edge of the plotting area, as shown in Figure 11-5. See Listing 11-5 for the SAS plot code.

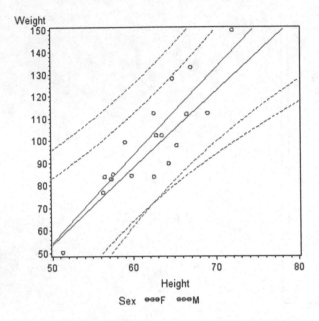

Figure 11-5. *Regression plot created by PROC GPLOT in SAS 9.2*

Listing 11-5. PROC GPLOT Regression Plot

```
PROC SORT DATA = sashelp.class
          OUT = class;
    BY sex height;
RUN;

PROC GPLOT DATA = class;
    SYMBOL V = CIRCLE I = ROCLI95;
    PLOT weight * height = sex;
RUN;
```

ODS Graphics from SAS 9.2 (Easy)

Again, there are fewer ticks on the two axes, and the minimum and maximum values on the axes are different to accommodate all the confidence-limit lines, whereas the SAS/GRAPH axis ranges are based on the data points. Unlike in the SAS/GRAPH plot, the confidence-limit lines in the ODS Graphics plot do not extend beyond the range of the data values on the x-axis, so no data extrapolation is carried out, as shown in Figure 11-6. See Listing 11-6 for the SAS plot code.

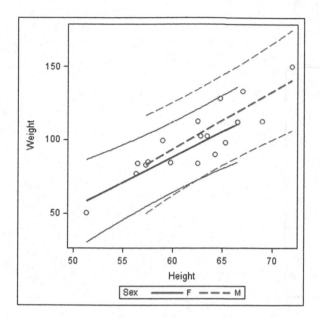

Figure 11-6. *Regression plot created by PROC SGPLOT in SAS 9.2*

Listing 11-6. PROC SGPLOT Regression Plot

```
PROC SORT DATA = sashelp.class
         OUT = class;
   BY sex height;
RUN;

PROC SGPLOT DATA = class;
   REG Y = weight X = height /
       GROUP = sex CLI
       MARKERATTRS = (SYMBOL=CIRCLE);
RUN;
```

Error Bar Plots

This type of plot is often created using a scatter plot and a fair amount of annotation. But in SAS/GRAPH, a little preprocessing of the input data lets you change the single data point into three points: original, upper error limit, and lower error limit, as shown in Figure 11-7. See Listing 11-7 for the SAS plot code.

SAS/GRAPH from SAS 9.2

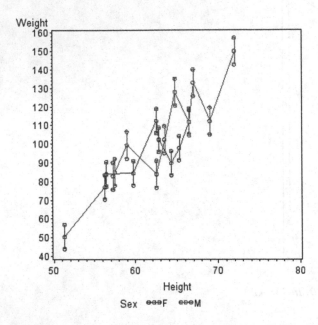

Figure 11-7. *Error bar plot created by PROC GPLOT in SAS 9.2*

Listing 11-7. PROC GPLOT Error Bar Plot

```
PROC SORT DATA = sashelp.class
         OUT = class;
    BY sex height;
RUN;

PROC SUMMARY DATA = class NWAY;
    CLASS sex;
    VAR weight;
    OUTPUT OUT = class_se
           STDERR = weight_se;
RUN;

DATA class_classic
    (KEEP = sex height value);
    MERGE class class_se;
    BY sex;
    value = weight;
    OUTPUT;
    value = weight + weight_se;
    OUTPUT;
    value = weight - weight_se;
    OUTPUT;
RUN;
```

```
PROC GPLOT DATA = class_classic;
    SYMBOL V = CIRCLE I = HILOTJ;
    PLOT value * height = sex;
    LABEL value = "Weight";
RUN;
```

ODS Graphics from SAS 9.2 (Easy)

ODS Graphics also requires a little preprocessing of the input data to add two extra values to each data point for the upper and lower error limits. This plot demonstrates an important feature of ODS Graphics: graphical elements can be drawn on top of previously drawn elements. In this case, the error bars are drawn using the SCATTER statement and then the line is drawn on top using the SERIES statement, so the error bars appear behind the line, as shown in Figure 11-8. See Listing 11-8 for the SAS plot code.

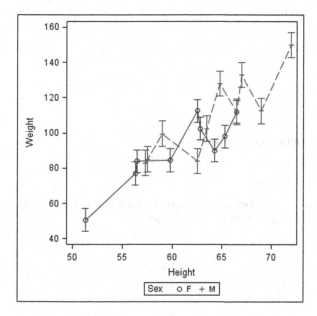

Figure 11-8. *Error bar plot created by PROC SGPLOT in SAS 9.2*

Listing 11-8. PROC SGPLOT *Error Bar Plot*

```
PROC SORT DATA = sashelp.class
        OUT = class;
    BY sex height;
RUN;

PROC SUMMARY DATA = class NWAY;
    CLASS sex;
    VAR weight;
    OUTPUT OUT = class_se
           STDERR = weight_se;
RUN;
```

```
DATA class_ods
    (KEEP = sex height value
           value_upper value_lower);
    MERGE class class_se;
    BY sex;
    value = weight;
    value_upper = weight + weight_se;
    value_lower = weight - weight_se;
    OUTPUT;
RUN;

PROC SGPLOT DATA = class_ods;
    SCATTER Y = value X = height /
        GROUP = sex
        YERRORUPPER = value_upper
        YERRORLOWER = value_lower;
    SERIES Y = value X = height /
        GROUP = sex;
    LABEL value = "Weight";
RUN;
```

Box Plots

You can use a box plot to display simple statistics, including quartiles and outliers.

SAS/GRAPH from SAS 9.2

The default SAS/GRAPH plot requires you to customize a number of features, such as the box width, to make it useful for the viewer, as shown in Figure 11-9. See Listing 11-9 for the SAS plot code.

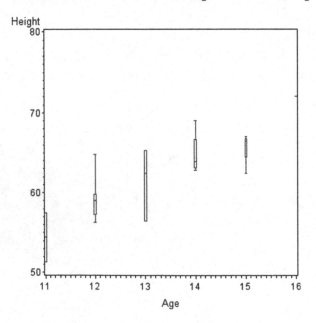

Figure 11-9. *Box plot created by PROC GPLOT in SAS 9.2*

Listing 11-9. `PROC GPLOT` Box Plot

```
PROC SORT DATA = sashelp.class
          OUT = class;
    BY age;
RUN;

PROC GPLOT DATA = class;
    SYMBOL I = BOXOOT;
    PLOT height * age;
RUN;
```

ODS Graphics from SAS 9.2 (Easy)

Using the default settings for ODS Graphics produces a box plot that is recognizably similar to that produced using the default settings in SAS/GRAPH, but the viewer can see the information in the graph much more clearly, as shown in Figure 11-10. See Listing 11-10 for the SAS plot code. The means are marked as diamond symbols and the medians as horizontal lines in the boxes, which mark the 25th and 75 percentiles. *Whiskers* (lines with T ends) indicate the 5th and 95th percentiles. *Outliers* (points outside the whiskers) are shown as circles.

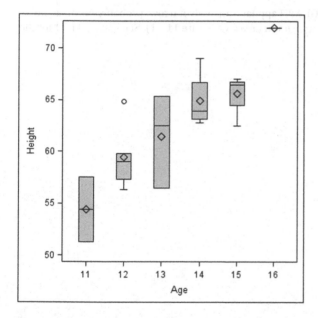

Figure 11-10. *Box plot created by* `PROC SGPLOT` *in SAS 9.2*

Listing 11-10. PROC SGPLOT Box Plot

```
PROC SORT DATA = sashelp.class
         OUT = class;
    BY age;
RUN;

PROC SGPLOT DATA = class;
    VBOX height / CATEGORY = age;
RUN;
```

Vertical Bar Charts

This is the first group of bar charts created by PROC GCHART in SAS/GRAPH. Each group includes a simple bar chart, a stacked bar chart (referred to as *subgrouped* in SAS/GRAPH), and a clustered bar chart (referred to as *grouped* in SAS/GRAPH). All the graphs in this chapter are drawn in square graph areas.

SAS/GRAPH from SAS 9.2

The simple and stacked bar charts drawn by SAS/GRAPH appear unusually narrow, probably because the default bar widths are fixed rather than adapted to the graph area (see Figure 11-11). See Listing 11-11 for the SAS plot code.

Simple Vertical Bar Chart

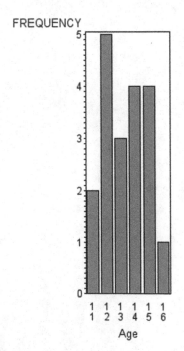

Figure 11-11. *Vertical bar chart created by PROC GCHART in SAS 9.2*

Listing 11-11. PROC GCHART Vertical Bar Chart

```
PROC GCHART DATA = class;
    VBAR age / DISCRETE;
RUN;
```

Stacked Vertical Bar Chart

The stacked version of the graph is also rather narrow, as shown in Figure 11-12. See Listing 11-12 for the SAS plot code.

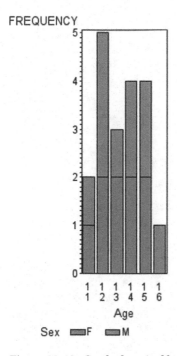

Figure 11-12. *Stacked vertical bar chart created by PROC GCHART in SAS 9.2*

Listing 11-12. PROC GCHART Stacked Vertical Bar Chart

```
PROC SORT DATA = sashelp.class
         OUT = class;
    BY sex age;
RUN;

PROC GCHART DATA = class;
    VBAR age / SUBGROUP = sex DISCRETE;
RUN;
```

Clustered Vertical Bar Chart

The clustered version is also narrow, as shown in Figure 11-13. See Listing 11-13 for the SAS plot code.

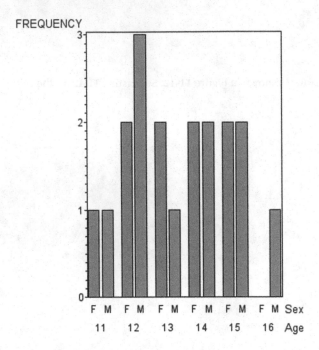

Figure 11-13. *Clustered vertical bar chart created by PROC GCHART in SAS 9.2*

Listing 11-13. PROC GCHART Clustered Vertical Bar Chart

```
PROC SORT DATA = sashelp.class
         OUT = class;
    BY sex age;
RUN;

PROC GCHART DATA = class;
    VBAR sex / GROUP = age
               PATTERNID = MIDPOINT;
RUN;
```

ODS Graphics from SAS 9.2 (Easy)

Vertical bar charts are available in the simple and stacked forms from SAS 9.2, where *stacked* is the new name for *subgrouped*.

Simple Vertical Bar Chart

The simple version is shown in Figure 11-14. See Listing 11-14 for the SAS plot code.

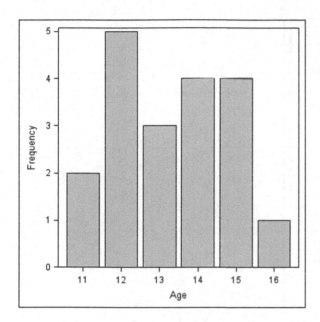

Figure 11-14. *Vertical bar chart created by PROC SGPLOT in SAS 9.2*

Listing 11-14. PROC SGPLOT Vertical Bar Chart

```
PROC SORT DATA = sashelp.class
         OUT = class;
    BY sex age;
RUN;

PROC SGPLOT DATA = class;
    VBAR age;
RUN;
```

Stacked Vertical Bar Chart

The stacked version is shown in Figure 11-15. See Listing 11-15 for the SAS plot code.

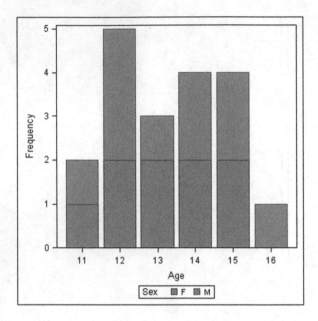

Figure 11-15. *Stacked vertical bar chart created by PROC SGPLOT in SAS 9.2*

Listing 11-15. PROC SGPLOT Stacked Vertical Bar Chart

```
PROC SORT DATA = sashelp.class
          OUT = class;
    BY sex age;
RUN;

PROC SGPLOT DATA = class;
    VBAR age / GROUP = sex;
RUN;
```

Clustered Vertical Bar Chart

The clustered form can only be approximated by using the paneled form in PROC SGPANEL. The simple version is shown in Figure 11-16. See Listing 11-16 for the SAS plot code. Note that the graph bars make full use of the available graph area!

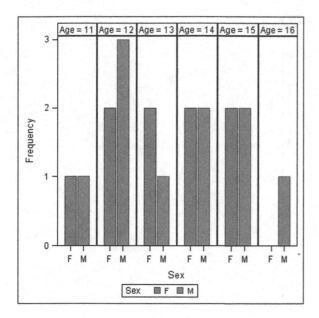

Figure 11-16. *Clustered vertical bar chart created by PROC SGPANEL in SAS 9.2*

Listing 11-16. PROC SGPANEL Clustered Vertical Bar Chart

```
PROC SORT DATA = sashelp.class
          OUT = class;
    BY sex age;
RUN;

PROC SGPANEL DATA = class;
    PANELBY age / COLUMNS = 6;
    VBAR sex / GROUP = sex;
RUN;
```

ODS Graphics from SAS 9.3 (Easy)

As of SAS 9.3, the clustered vertical bar chart is supported using the GROUPDISPLAY = CLUSTER option, so the paneled form is no longer necessary. However, the bars are identified solely via the legend, as is the case for the stacked bar chart, as shown in Figure 11-17. See Listing 11-17 for the SAS plot code.

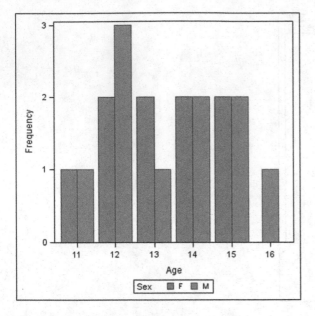

Figure 11-17. *Clustered vertical bar chart created by PROC SGPLOT in SAS 9.3*

Listing 11-17. PROC SGPLOT Clustered Vertical Bar Chart

```
PROC SORT DATA = sashelp.class
         OUT = class;
   BY sex age;
RUN;

PROC SGPLOT DATA = class;
   VBAR age / GROUP = sex
             GROUPDISPLAY = CLUSTER;
RUN;
```

Horizontal Bar Charts

The default horizontal bar chart in SAS/GRAPH includes statistics on the right side of the chart. This feature creates the biggest problem when attempting to replicate this chart in ODS Graphics.

SAS/GRAPH from SAS 9.2

Note that the default horizontal bar charts, unlike the vertical bar charts, make full use of the available graph area.

Simple Horizontal Bar Chart

The simple version is shown in Figure 11-18. See Listing 11-18 for the SAS plot code.

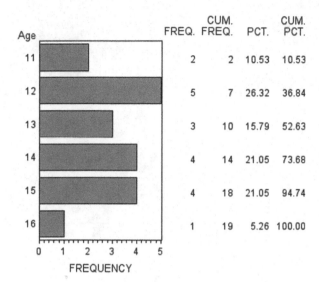

Figure 11-18. *Horizontal bar chart created by PROC GCHART in SAS 9.2*

Listing 11-18. PROC GCHART Horizontal Bar Chart

```
PROC SORT DATA = sashelp.class
         OUT = class;
    BY sex age;
RUN;

PROC GCHART DATA = class;
    HBAR age / DISCRETE;
RUN;
```

Stacked Horizontal Bar Chart

The stacked version is shown in Figure 11-19. See Listing 11-19 for the SAS plot code.

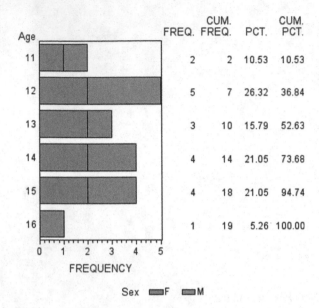

Age	FREQ.	CUM. FREQ.	PCT.	CUM. PCT.
11	2	2	10.53	10.53
12	5	7	26.32	36.84
13	3	10	15.79	52.63
14	4	14	21.05	73.68
15	4	18	21.05	94.74
16	1	19	5.26	100.00

Figure 11-19. Stacked horizontal bar chart created by PROC GCHART in SAS 9.2

Listing 11-19. PROC GCHART Stacked Horizontal Bar Chart

```
PROC SORT DATA = sashelp.class
         OUT = class;
    BY sex age;
RUN;

PROC GCHART DATA = class;
    HBAR age / SUBGROUP = sex DISCRETE;
RUN;
```

Clustered Horizontal Bar Chart

The clustered version is shown in Figure 11-20. See Listing 11-20 for the SAS plot code.

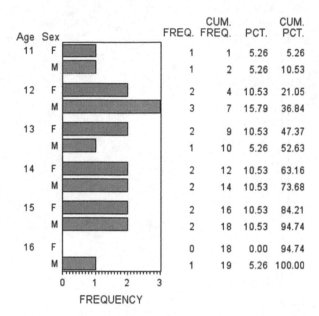

Figure 11-20. *Clustered horizontal bar chart created by PROC GCHART in SAS 9.2*

Listing 11-20. PROC GCHART Clustered Horizontal Bar Chart

```
PROC SORT DATA = sashelp.class
         OUT = class;
   BY sex age;
RUN;

PROC GCHART DATA = class;
   HBAR sex / GROUP = age
              PATTERNID = MIDPOINT;
RUN;
```

ODS Graphics from SAS 9.2 (Easy)

If you just want to create a horizontal bar chart in the form of a rotated vertical bar chart, you can do so in SAS 9.2 for the simple and stacked forms. However, the statistics on the right side of the bar chart are not added here, because doing so requires extensive PROC TEMPLATE code to plot text versions of the statistics in separate layouts.

Simple Horizontal Bar Chart

The simple form is shown in Figure 11-21. See Listing 11-21 for the SAS plot code.

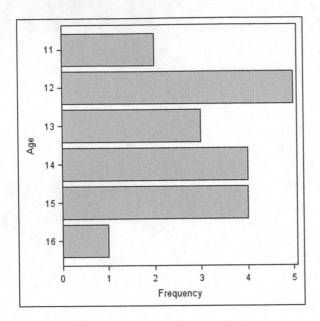

Figure 11-21. *Horizontal bar chart created by PROC SGPLOT in SAS 9.2*

Listing 11-21. PROC SGPLOT Horizontal Bar Chart

```
PROC SORT DATA = sashelp.class
         OUT = class;
    BY sex age;
RUN;

PROC SGPLOT DATA = class;
    HBAR age;
RUN;
```

Stacked Horizontal Bar Chart

The stacked version is shown in Figure 11-22. See Listing 11-22 for the SAS plot code.

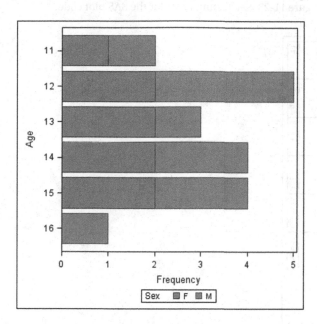

Figure 11-22. *Stacked horizontal bar chart created by PROC SGPLOT in SAS 9.2*

Listing 11-22. PROC SGPLOT Stacked Horizontal Bar Chart

```
PROC SORT DATA = sashelp.class
          OUT = class;
    BY sex age;
RUN;

PROC SGPLOT DATA = class;
    HBAR age / GROUP = sex;
RUN;
```

Clustered Horizontal Bar Chart

The clustered version of the horizontal bar chart is not possible directly in SAS 9.2, but you can create an approximation using PROC SGPANEL, as shown in Figure 11-23. See Listing 11-23 for the SAS plot code.

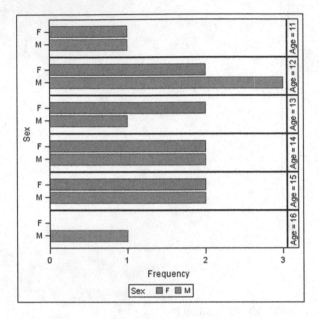

Figure 11-23. *Clustered horizontal bar chart created by PROC SGPANEL in SAS 9.2*

Listing 11-23. PROC SGPANEL Clustered Horizontal Bar Chart

```
PROC SORT DATA = sashelp.class
         OUT = class;
   BY sex age;
RUN;

PROC SGPANEL DATA = class;
   PANELBY age / ROWS = 6;
   HBAR sex / GROUP = sex;
RUN;
```

ODS Graphics from SAS 9.3 (Easy)

As of SAS 9.3, the clustered horizontal bar chart is supported using the GROUPDISPLAY = CLUSTER option, so the paneled form is no longer necessary, as shown in Figure 11-24. See Listing 11-24 for the SAS plot code. The bars are identified solely via the legend, as is the case for the stacked bar chart.

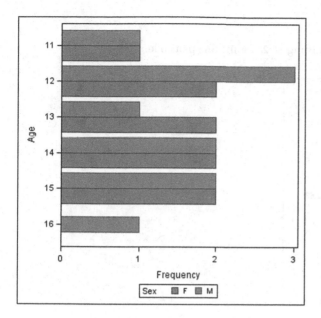

Figure 11-24. *Clustered horizontal bar chart created by PROC SGPLOT in SAS 9.3*

Listing 11-24. PROC SGPLOT Clustered Horizontal Bar Chart

```
PROC SORT DATA = sashelp.class
          OUT = class;
    BY sex age;
RUN;

PROC SGPLOT DATA = class;
    HBAR age / GROUP = sex
               GROUPDISPLAY = CLUSTER;
RUN;
```

ODS Graphics from SAS 9.4 (Difficult and Impossible)

As of SAS 9.4, the YAXISTABLE statement in PROC SGPLOT lets you align text and bars, but only for the primary midpoint axis in SAS 9.4 and 9.4M1, not for the clustering axis. Thus only single rows of text can be included. The ability to align text with the clustering axis is expected to be included in SAS 9.4M2. The data needs to be carefully prepared before rendering, which makes it much less convenient to use than the HBAR statement in PROC GCHART.

Simple Horizontal Bar Chart

The simple version is shown in Figure 11-25. See Listing 11-25 for the SAS plot code.

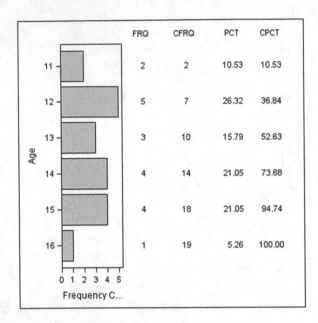

Figure 11-25. *Horizontal bar chart created by PROC SGPLOT in SAS 9.4*

Listing 11-25. PROC SGPLOT Horizontal Bar Chart

```
PROC SORT DATA = sashelp.class
         OUT = class;
   BY age;
RUN;

PROC FREQ DATA = class;
   TABLES age /
         OUT = class_summ NOPRINT;
RUN;

DATA class_summ;
   SET class_summ;
   BY age;
   RETAIN cum_freq cum_pct .;
   freq = count;
   cum_freq + count;
   cum_pct + percent;
   FORMAT freq cum_freq 3.
          percent cum_pct 6.2;
   LABEL freq = 'FRQ'
         cum_freq = 'CFRQ'
         percent = 'PCT'
         cum_pct = 'CPCT';
RUN;
```

```
PROC SGPLOT DATA = class_summ;
    HBAR age / STAT = FREQ;
    YAXISTABLE freq cum_freq
                percent cum_pct /
        LOCATION = INSIDE
        POSITION = RIGHT
        LABELPOS = TOP;
RUN;
```

Stacked Horizontal Bar Chart

The stacked version is shown in Figure 11-26. See Listing 11-26 for the SAS plot code.

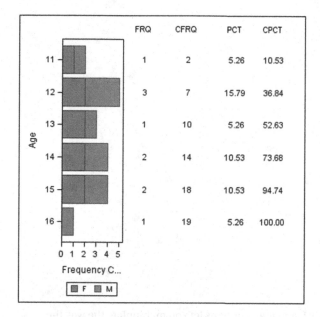

Figure 11-26. *Stacked horizontal bar chart created by PROC SGPLOT in SAS 9.4*

Listing 11-26. PROC SGPLOT Stacked Horizontal Bar Chart

```
PROC SORT DATA = sashelp.class
        OUT = class;
    BY sex age;
RUN;

PROC FREQ DATA = class;
    TABLES sex * age /
        OUT = class_stack_summ NOPRINT;
RUN;

DATA class_stack_summ;
    SET class_stack_summ;
    BY sex age;
    RETAIN cum_freq cum_pct .;
```

```
        freq = count;
        cum_freq + count;
        cum_pct + percent;
        FORMAT freq cum_freq 3.
                percent cum_pct 6.2;
        LABEL freq = 'FRQ'
            cum_freq = 'CFRQ'
            percent = 'PCT'
            cum_pct = 'CPCT';
RUN;

DATA class_stack_summ;
    SET class_stack_summ;
    BY sex age;
    IF NOT LAST.age THEN DO;
        freq = .;
        cum_freq = .;
        percent = .;
        cum_pct = .;
    END;
RUN;

PROC SGPLOT DATA = class_stack_summ;
    HBAR age / GROUP = sex;
    YAXISTABLE freq cum_freq
                percent cum_pct /
        LOCATION = INSIDE
        POSITION = RIGHT
        LABELPOS = TOP;
RUN;
```

2D Pie Charts

2D pie charts are simple to create using SAS/GRAPH, and many options let you manipulate the way the segments and labels are presented. The example code is deliberately very simple.

SAS/GRAPH from SAS 9.2

A 2D pie chart is very easy to create using PROC GCHART in SAS 9.2, as shown in Figure 11-27. See Listing 11-27 for the SAS plot code.

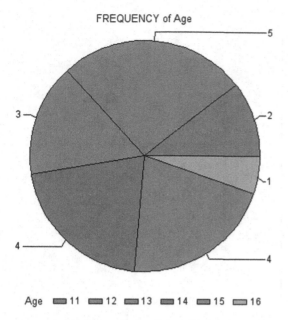

Figure 11-27. *2D pie chart created by PROC GCHART in SAS 9.2*

Listing 11-27. PROC GCHART 2D Pie Chart

```
PROC SORT DATA = sashelp.class
          OUT = class;
    BY age;
RUN;

PROC GCHART DATA = class;
    PIE age / VALUE = ARROW
              LEGEND DISCRETE;
RUN;
```

ODS Graphics in SAS 9.2 (Impossible)

2D pie charts are not available in the SG procedures, nor in PROC TEMPLATE, in SAS 9.2.

ODS Graphics as of SAS 9.3 (Difficult)

2D pie charts are available in PROC TEMPLATE, but not in the SG procedures, as of SAS 9.3. The ODS Graphics sample has been deliberately plotted with the segments in a clockwise direction from 9:00, instead of counterclockwise from 3:00 as in the SAS/GRAPH code, to emphasize the differences, as shown in Figure 11-28. See Listing 11-28 for the SAS plot code.

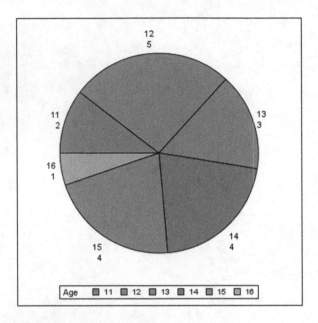

Figure 11-28. 2D pie chart created by PROC TEMPLATE with PROC SGRENDER in SAS 9.3

Listing 11-28. PROC TEMPLATE 2D Pie Chart

```
PROC SORT DATA = sashelp.class
         OUT = class;
    BY age;
RUN;

PROC TEMPLATE;
  DEFINE STATGRAPH pie;
    BEGINGRAPH;
      LAYOUT REGION;
        PIECHART CATEGORY = age /
          DATALABELLOCATION = OUTSIDE
          CATEGORYDIRECTION = CLOCKWISE
          START = 180 NAME = 'pie';
        DISCRETELEGEND 'pie' /
          TITLE = 'Age';
      ENDLAYOUT;
    ENDGRAPH;
  END;
RUN;

PROC SGRENDER DATA = class
         TEMPLATE = pie;
RUN;
```

3D Pie Charts

I have never really liked this chart. My opinion is that, rather than informing the viewer, such graphics are frequently used to mislead the viewer. As a consequence, I have not included any SAS/GRAPH example code here.

ODS Graphics in SAS 9.2, 9.3, and 9.4 (Impossible)

It is with great delight that I have discovered that 3D pie charts will not be supported in any release of ODS Graphics in the near future. This does not prevent SAS users who wish to create these charts from doing so, but they will be required to license SAS/GRAPH first.

Conclusions

If you are reading this chapter with a view to converting all of your SAS graphics programs from SAS/GRAPH to ODS Graphics, you must consider the following questions:

- Do you only create plots, and no charts? This means your programs can probably be converted from SAS/GRAPH to ODS Graphics in SAS 9.2 or 9.3, provided any annotation that is currently used can be plotted as another plot to be overlaid over the base plot.

- If you create bar charts, do you draw horizontal bar charts that require large amounts of text alongside? If the bar charts (vertical or horizontal) require only a single value plotted in or at the end of the bar, you should be able to convert your programs from SAS/GRAPH to ODS Graphics in SAS 9.2 or 9.3, although some PROC TEMPLATE code may be necessary for more complex charts.

- If you require horizontal clustered bar charts with large amounts of text added, or 2D or 3D pie charts, then it may not be possible to convert your SAS/GRAPH programs to ODS Graphics, even in SAS 9.4—or, at best, you may be able to do so with a great deal of effort. It is recommended that you keep your SAS/GRAPH license for now, because PROC GCHART is not going away in the foreseeable future!

Recommended Reading

- Philip R. Holland, *Graphs: How Do You Do This in SAS?* (Holland Numerics Ltd., 2013), https://sites.google.com/site/hnlsas/apps/howsas03.

- Sanjay Matange and Dan Heath, *Statistical Graphics Procedures by Example: Effective Graphs Using SAS* (SAS Institute, 2011).

- Sanjay Matange, *Getting Started with the Graph Template Language in SAS: Examples, Tips, and Techniques for Creating Custom Graphs* (SAS Institute, 2013).

- Sanjay Matange, *Graphically Speaking* (blog), http://blogs.sas.com/content/graphicallyspeaking.

CHAPTER 12

■ ■ ■

Converting SAS/GRAPH Annotate to ODS Graphics

The previous chapter described how many standard SAS/GRAPH plots can be converted easily to ODS Graphics by using simple `PROC SGPLOT` or `PROC SGPANEL` code. SAS/GRAPH Annotate code would seem, at first glance, to be much more difficult to convert to ODS Graphics; but by making use of its layering features, many Annotate plots can be replicated in a flexible and repeatable way.

This chapter compares the output from commonly used Annotate and SAS/GRAPH code for producing annotated graphs with equivalent code that uses only ODS Graphics. Each ODS Graphics program is rated as follows:

- *Easy*: One Annotate data set and one SAS/GRAPH procedure statement can be replaced with an ODS Graphics procedure. The conversion may also require some simple preprocessing of the input data.

- *Difficult*: One Annotate data set and one SAS/GRAPH procedure can be replaced with code containing `PROC TEMPLATE` and `PROC SGRENDER`, or the conversion requires extensive preprocessing of the input data.

- *Impossible*: There is currently no corresponding ODS Graphics procedure in that version of SAS software to replicate the Annotate and SAS/GRAPH plot. However, the annotated plots selected for this chapter can all be created using ODS Graphics, so none of them are rated Impossible.

Each plot is followed by the SAS code used to create it and is identified in in the text.

Error Bars

Error-bar plots are used extensively in clinical trials to display collected data—such as laboratory test results over time—and demonstrate the effect, or lack of effect, caused by the study drug. This type of plot is often created using a scatter plot and a fair amount of annotation.

The sample data for SAS/GRAPH (class_error_classic) and ODS Graphics (class_error_ods) is generated using the following code:

```
PROC SORT DATA = sashelp.class OUT = class_error;
    BY sex height;
RUN;

PROC SUMMARY DATA = class_error NWAY;
    CLASS sex;
    VAR weight;
    OUTPUT OUT = class_error_se STDERR = weight_se;
RUN;

DATA class_error_classic (KEEP = sex height value)
     class_error_ods (KEEP = sex height value value_upper value_lower)
     ;
    MERGE class_error class_error_se;
    BY sex;
    value = weight;
    value_upper = value + weight_se;
    value_lower = value - weight_se;
    OUTPUT class_error_ods;
    OUTPUT class_error_classic;
    value = value_upper;
    OUTPUT class_error_classic;
    value = value_lower;
    OUTPUT class_error_classic;
RUN;
```

SAS/GRAPH from SAS 9.2

You can create error-bar plots using PROC GPLOT and Annotate, instead of the HILOTJ interpolation used in the previous chapter, as shown in Figure 12-1. See Listing 12-1 for the SAS plot code.

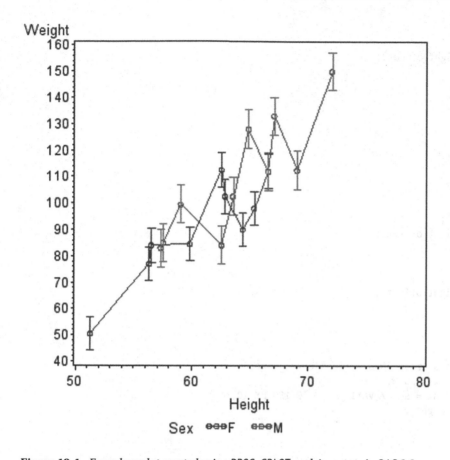

Figure 12-1. *Error-bar plot created using* PROC GPLOT *and Annotate in SAS 9.2*

Listing 12-1. PROC GPLOT Error-Bar Plot

```
%LET height_offset = 0.3;

DATA class_error_anno;
    SET class_error_ods;
    BY sex;
    LENGTH function $8
           color $20
           when xsys ysys $1
           x y 8
           ;
    xsys = '2';
    ysys = '2';
    when = 'A';
    IF sex = 'M' THEN color = 'RED';
    ELSE color = 'BLUE';
    function = 'MOVE';
    x = height - &height_offset.;
    y = value_upper;
```

```
    OUTPUT;
    function = 'DRAW';
    x = height + &height_offset.;
    y = value_upper;
    OUTPUT;
    function = 'MOVE';
    x = height;
    y = value_upper;
    OUTPUT;
    function = 'DRAW';
    x = height;
    y = value_lower;
    OUTPUT;
    function = 'MOVE';
    x = height - &height_offset.;
    y = value_lower;
    OUTPUT;
    function = 'DRAW';
    x = height + &height_offset.;
    y = value_lower;
    OUTPUT;
RUN;

PROC GPLOT DATA = class_error ANNO = class_error_anno;
    SYMBOL V = CIRCLE I = JOIN;
    PLOT weight * height = sex / VAXIS = 40 TO 160 BY 10;
    LABEL weight = "Weight";
RUN;
```

ODS Graphics from SAS 9.2 (Easy)

As you saw in the previous chapter, the error bars are drawn using the YERRORUPPER= and YERRORLOWER= parameters, as shown in Figure 12-2. See Listing 12-2 for the SAS plot code.

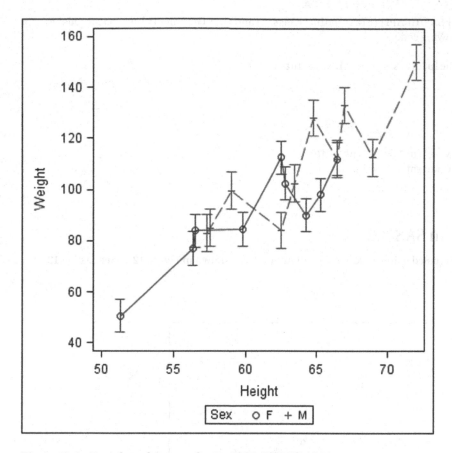

Figure 12-2. *Error-bar plot created using* PROC SGPLOT *in SAS 9.2*

Listing 12-2. PROC SGPLOT Error-Bar Plot

```
PROC SGPLOT DATA = class_error_ods;
    SCATTER Y = value X = height / GROUP = sex YERRORUPPER = value_upper
                                    YERRORLOWER = value_lower;
    SERIES Y = value X = height / GROUP = sex;
    LABEL value = "Weight";
RUN;
```

Point Labels

It is frequently useful to label specific points in a scatter plot so that the individual points can be identified. In this example, all the points are labeled; you may not need to label every point in other circumstances, so you could instead label just a subset of points with important features.

The sample data for SAS/GRAPH (class_point_classic) and ODS Graphics (class_point_ods) is generated using the following code:

```
PROC SORT DATA = sashelp.class OUT = class_point;
    BY sex height;
RUN;

DATA class_point_ods;
    SET class_point;
    If sex = 'F' THEN weight2 = weight + 10;
                 ELSE weight2 = weight - 10;
RUN;
```

SAS/GRAPH from SAS 9.2

Point-label plots can be created using PROC GPLOT and Annotate, as shown in Figure 12-3. See Listing 12-3 for the SAS plot code.

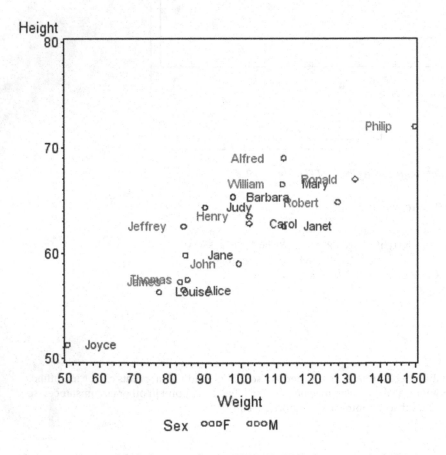

Figure 12-3. *Point-label plot created using PROC GPLOT and Annotate in SAS 9.2*

190

Listing 12-3. PROC GPLOT Point-Label Plot

```
DATA class_point_anno;
    SET class_point_ods;
    BY sex;
    LENGTH function $8
            color $20
            position when xsys ysys hsys $1
            x y size 8
            ;
    xsys = '2';
    ysys = '2';
    hsys = 'D';
    when = 'A';
    size = '8';
    IF sex = 'M' THEN color = 'RED';
    ELSE color = 'BLUE';
    function = 'LABEL';
    x = weight2;
    y = height;
    text = name;
    position = '+';
    OUTPUT;
RUN;

PROC GPLOT DATA = class_point ANNO = class_point_anno;
    SYMBOL V = CIRCLE;
    PLOT height * weight = sex;
RUN;
```

ODS Graphics from SAS 9.2 (Easy)

Point labels are plotted using a second SCATTER statement, as shown in Figure 12-4. See Listing 12-4 for the SAS plot code.

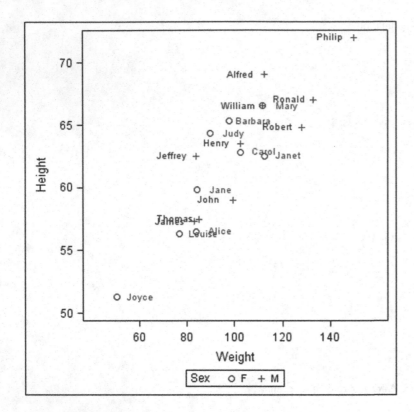

Figure 12-4. *Point-label plot created using PROC SGPLOT in SAS 9.2*

Listing 12-4. PROC SGPLOT Point-Label Plot

```
PROC SGPLOT DATA = class_point_ods;
    SCATTER Y = height X = weight / GROUP = sex;
    SCATTER Y = height X = weight2 / GROUP = sex MARKERCHAR = name;
RUN;
```

Bar Labels

You can label bars with simple plot options in SAS/GRAPH, but labeling individual bar segments in a stacked bar chart with SAS/GRAPH requires Annotate code. The sample data for SAS/GRAPH (class_bar) and ODS Graphics (class_bar_ods) is generated using the following code:

```
PROC SUMMARY DATA = sashelp.class NWAY;
    CLASS age sex;
    VAR height;
    OUTPUT OUT = class_bar N = count;
RUN;

DATA class_bar_ods;
    SET class_bar;
    BY age sex;
```

```
    LENGTH ccount $1;
    RETAIN total_count .;
    ccount = STRIP(PUT(count, 1.));
    IF FIRST.age THEN DO;
        total_count = 0;
        count_ods = count - 0.5;
    END;
    ELSE DO;
        count_ods = count;
    END;
    total_count + count;
    total_count_ods = total_count - 0.5;
    IF sex = 'F' THEN total_count_odsf = total_count_ods;
    ELSE total_count_odsm = total_count_ods;
RUN;
```

SAS/GRAPH from SAS 9.2

Bar-label plots can be created using PROC GCHART and Annotate, as shown in Figure 12-5. See Listing 12-5 for the SAS plot code.

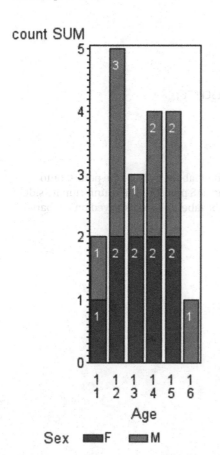

Figure 12-5. Bar-label plot created using PROC GCHART and Annotate in SAS 9.2

Listing 12-5. PROC GCHART Bar-Label Plot

```
DATA class_bar_anno;
    SET class_bar_ods;
    BY age sex;
    LENGTH function $8
           color $20
           position when xsys ysys hsys $1
           x y size 8
           ;
    xsys = '2';
    ysys = '2';
    hsys = 'D';
    when = 'A';
    size = '8';
    color = 'WHITE';
    function = 'LABEL';
    x = age;
    y = total_count;
    text = ccount;
    position = '8';
    OUTPUT;
RUN;

PROC GCHART DATA = class_bar ANNO = class_bar_anno;
    PATTERN1 VALUE = SOLID COLOR = BLUE;
    PATTERN2 VALUE = SOLID COLOR = RED;
    VBAR age / SUBGROUP = sex TYPE = SUM SUMVAR = count DISCRETE;
RUN;
```

ODS Graphics from SAS 9.3 (Easy)

The following example uses the VLINE statement to plot a series of point labels, without the points, onto the vertical bar chart, as shown in Figure 12-6 (see Listing 12-6 for the SAS plot code). The unfortunate side effect of this technique is that there is no absolute guarantee where the label will be displayed on the bars.

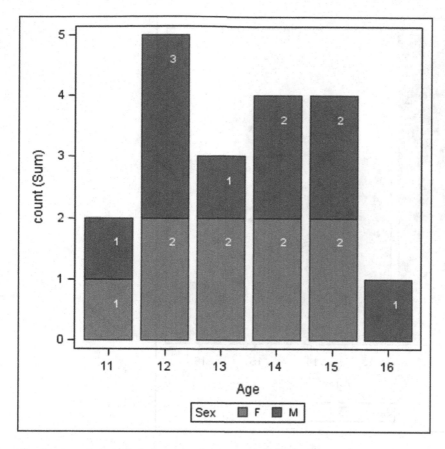

Figure 12-6. Point-label plot created using PROC SGPLOT in SAS 9.3

Listing 12-6. PROC SGPLOT Point-Label Plot

```
PROC SGPLOT DATA = class_bar_ods;
    VBAR age / GROUP = sex GROUPORDER = ASCENDING RESPONSE = count STAT = SUM;
    VLINE age / GROUP = sex GROUPORDER = ASCENDING RESPONSE = total_count_ods STAT = SUM
                DATALABEL = ccount DATALABELPOS = DATA
                DATALABELATTRS = (COLOR = WHITE WEIGHT = BOLD)
                LINEATTRS = (THICKNESS = 0);
RUN;
```

ODS Graphics from SAS 9.4 (Easy)

SAS 9.4 introduces the SEGLABEL option for VBAR, which lets you place labels in the center of any bar segment, as shown in Figure 12-7. See Listing 12-7 for the SAS plot code.

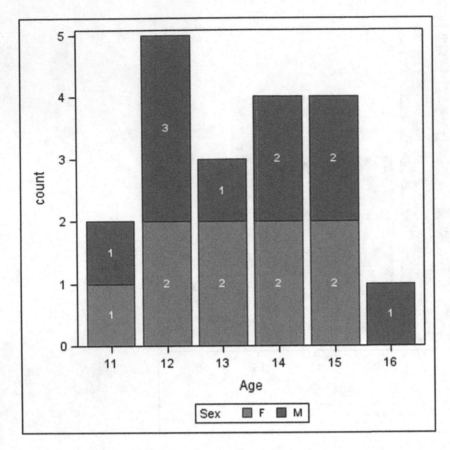

Figure 12-7. *Point-label plot created using PROC SGPLOT in SAS 9.4.*

Listing 12-7. PROC SGPLOT Point-Label Plot

```
PROC SGPLOT DATA = class_bar_ods;
    VBARPARM CATEGORY = age RESPONSE = count / GROUP = sex GROUPORDER = ASCENDING
                                               GROUPDISPLAY = STACK DATALABEL = count
                                               DATALABELPOS = DATA SEGLABEL
                                               SEGLABELATTRS = (COLOR = WHITE WEIGHT = BOLD);
RUN;
```

Information Boxes

Information boxes are vital to add necessary textual data to graphs. Being able to generate the text and data as part of the graph program helps ensure that the information displayed is relevant.

The sample data for SAS/GRAPH and ODS Graphics (class_info and class_info_range) is generated using the following code:

```
PROC SORT DATA = sashelp.class OUT = class_info;
    BY height weight;
RUN;

PROC SUMMARY DATA = class_info NWAY;
    VAR height weight;
    OUTPUT OUT = class_info_range MIN = min_height min_weight MAX = max_height max_weight;
RUN;
```

SAS/GRAPH from SAS 9.2

Information-box plots can be created using PROC GPLOT and Annotate, as shown in Figure 12-8. See Listing 12-8 for the SAS plot code.

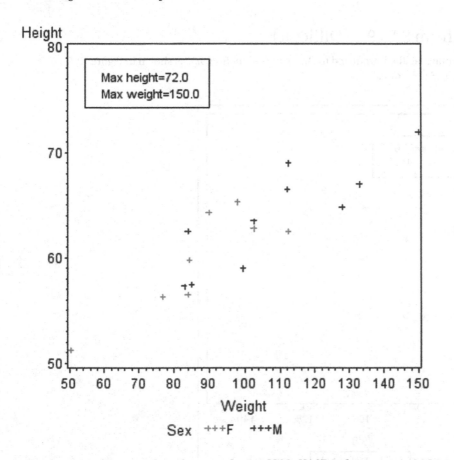

Figure 12-8. Information-box plot created using PROC GPLOT and Annotate in SAS 9.2

Listing 12-8. PROC GPLOT Information-Box Plot

```
DATA class_info_anno (DROP = min_: max_: _:);
    SET class_info_range;
    %dclanno;
    LENGTH text $50;
    xsys = '1';
    ysys = '1';
    hsys = '3';
    when = 'A';
    %RECT(5, 95, 40, 80, BLACK, 1, 1);
    %LABEL(10, 90, "Max height=" || STRIP(PUT(max_height, 8.1)), BLACK, 0, 0, 3, Arial, 6);
    %LABEL(10, 85, "Max weight=" || STRIP(PUT(max_weight, 8.1)), BLACK, 0, 0, 3, Arial, 6);
RUN;

PROC GPLOT DATA = class_info ANNO = class_info_anno;
    PLOT height * weight = sex;
RUN;
```

ODS Graphics from SAS 9.3 (Difficult)

This code uses the Annotate facility introduced to ODS Graphics in SAS 9.3, as shown in Figure 12-9. See Listing 12-9 for the SAS plot code.

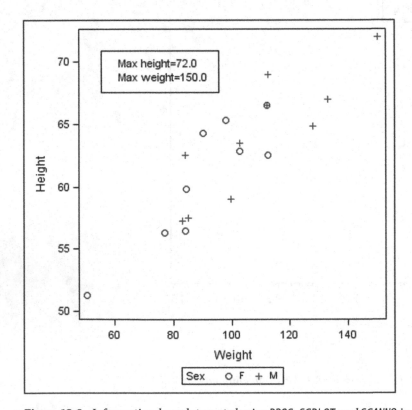

Figure 12-9. *Information-box plot created using PROC SGPLOT and SGANNO in SAS 9.3*

Listing 12-9. PROC SGPLOT Information Box Plot

```
DATA class_info_sganno (DROP = min_: max_: _:);
    SET class_info_range;
    LENGTH label $50;
    drawspace = 'DATAPERCENT';
    width = 40;
    anchor = 'TOPLEFT';
    function = 'RECTANGLE';
    height = 15;
    x1 = 5;
    y1 = 95;
    linecolor = 'BLACK';
    linethickness = 1;
    OUTPUT;
    anchor = 'LEFT';
    textsize = 8;
    height = .;
    function = 'TEXT';
    label = "Max height=" || STRIP(PUT(max_height, 8.1));
    x1 = 10;
    y1 = 90;
    OUTPUT;
    function = 'TEXT';
    label = "Max weight=" || STRIP(PUT(max_weight, 8.1));
    x1 = 10;
    y1 = 85;
    OUTPUT;
RUN;

PROC SGPLOT DATA = class_info SGANNO = class_info_sganno;
    SCATTER X = weight Y = height / GROUP = sex;
RUN;
```

ODS Graphics from SAS 9.2 (Difficult)

If you prefer to use the layering techniques in ODS Graphics, you can achieve the same annotation by plotting the information box and the text inside as separate overlaid plots, as shown in Figure 12-10. See Listing 12-10 for the SAS plot code.

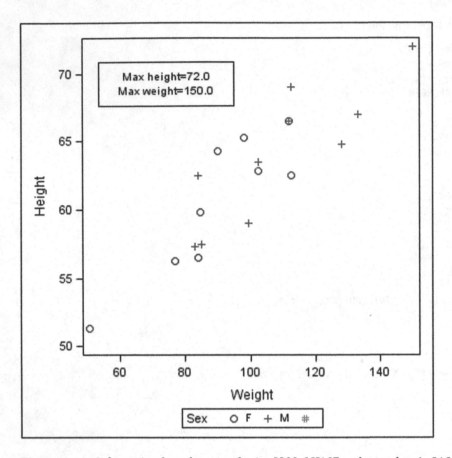

Figure 12-10. *Information-box plot created using PROC SGPLOT and extra data in SAS 9.2*

Listing 12-10. PROC SGPLOT Information-Box Plot

```
DATA class_info_box (DROP = min_: max_: _:);
    SET class_info_range;
    LENGTH text $50;
    xbox = 5;
    ybox = 95;
    OUTPUT;
    xbox = 45;
    ybox = 95;
    OUTPUT;
    xbox = 45;
    ybox = 80;
    OUTPUT;
    xbox = 5;
    ybox = 80;
    OUTPUT;
    xbox = 5;
    ybox = 95;
    OUTPUT;
```

```
        xbox = .;
        ybox = .;
        xtext = 25;
        ytext = 90;
        text = "Max height=" || STRIP(PUT(max_height, 8.1));
        OUTPUT;
        xtext = 25;
        ytext = 85;
        text = "Max weight=" || STRIP(PUT(max_weight, 8.1));
        OUTPUT;
RUN;

DATA class_info_ods;
    SET class_info
        class_info_box
        ;
RUN;

PROC SGPLOT DATA = class_info_ods;
    SCATTER X = weight Y = height / GROUP = sex;
    SERIES X = xbox Y = ybox / LINEATTRS = (COLOR = BLACK) X2AXIS Y2AXIS;
    SCATTER X = xtext Y = ytext / MARKERCHAR = text MARKERCHARATTRS = (COLOR = BLACK)
                                  X2AXIS Y2AXIS;
    XAXIS OFFSETMIN = 0.02 OFFSETMAX = 0.02;
    X2AXIS OFFSETMIN = 0 OFFSETMAX = 0 MIN = 0 MAX = 100
           DISPLAY = (NOLABEL NOTICKS NOVALUES);
    Y2AXIS MIN = 0 MAX = 100 DISPLAY = (NOLABEL NOTICKS NOVALUES);
RUN;
```

ODS Graphics from SAS 9.2 (Easy)

There is an ODS Graphics plotting statement that can create an information box, but it requires you to set up a specific syntax in a macro variable, as shown in Figure 12-11. See Listing 12-11 for the SAS plot code.

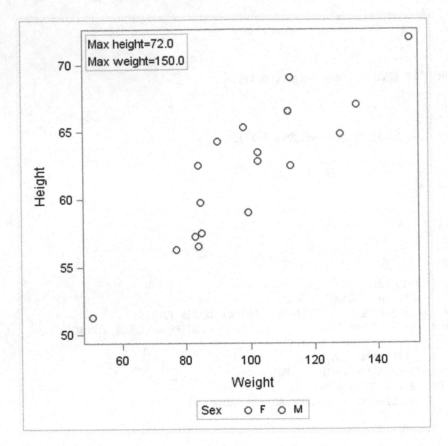

Figure 12-11. *Information-box plot created using PROC SGPLOT and the INSET statement in SAS 9.2*

Listing 12-11. PROC SGPLOT Information-Box Plot

```
DATA _NULL_;
  SET class_info_range;
  CALL SYMPUT('inset', '"Max height=' || STRIP(PUT(max_height, 8.1)) || '"' ||
                        ' ' ||
                        '"Max weight=' || STRIP(PUT(max_weight, 8.1)) || '"');
RUN;

PROC SGPLOT DATA = class_info;
    SCATTER X = weight Y = height / GROUP = sex;
    INSET &inset. / BORDER POSITION = TOPLEFT;
RUN;
```

Conclusions

Generating plots using ODS Graphics is based on the very simple application of graph layers, where individual graphs are drawn on top of each other to create the finished plot:

- Error bars can be generated by plotting a SCATTER plot with YERRORUPPER= and YERRORLOWER= options on top of, or below, a SERIES plot from SAS 9.2.

- Point labels can be generated by plotting the labels with a second SCATTER plot with MARKERCHAR options for the text, where the x-coordinates are offset to improve readability from SAS 9.2.

- Bar labels can be generated by plotting the labels with a VLINE plot on top of a VBAR chart in SAS 9.3, although the positioning of the labels may be offset slightly. In SAS 9.4, you can generate bar labels more precisely by using SEGLABEL options with a VBARPARM chart.

- Information boxes can be generated with the SGANNO= option of PROC SGPLOT in SAS 9.3, which is the ODS Graphics equivalent of Annotate. However, by calculating the location of the box corners and the text, you can draw a similar information box with more flexibility in SAS 9.2 using a simple input data set containing extra data coordinates, an extra SERIES statement for the box, and an extra SCATTER statement with MARKERCHAR options for the text. The final alternative is to build the information box in a macro variable and use an INSET statement to render it.

CHAPTER 13

■ ■ ■

Customizing Graph Templates

Previous chapters have discussed a variety of methods for generating graph templates. However, most of the generated templates are usable only for specific applications, rather than for multiple uses. This chapter goes more deeply into the structure and syntax of graph templates, so you can update the generated templates to make them more generally applicable.

Structure and Syntax

It is a fact of life for template programmers that until you are aware of what templates can do, you will struggle to develop useful template programs. The following sections explain the structure of graph templates and then expand on the syntax.

Structure

The basic Graph Template Language (GTL) is made up of nested structures, including LAYOUT statements and PLOT statements. The nested structure of a graph template is illustrated in Figure 13-1.

```
PROC TEMPLATE;
 DEFINE STATGRAPH name; /*create the template*/
 DYNAMIC name(s);  /*define any parameters (optional)*/
 MVAR name(s); /*define character macro variables used by name (optional)*/
 NMVAR name(s); /*define numeric macro variables used by name (optional)*/

 BEGINGRAPH; /*start the graph (new in SAS 9.2!)*/
  ENTRYTITLE title; /*create a title (repeated for additional titles)*/

   LAYOUT /*at least one layout statement is required*/

    LAYOUT  /*nested layout statements (optional)*/

     Any plot statements, including titles, graph areas, footnotes, etc.

    ENDLAYOUT;

     Any plot statements, including titles, graph areas, footnotes, etc.

   ENDLAYOUT;

  ENTRYFOOTNOTE footnote;  /*create a footnote (repeated for additional footnotes)*/
  ENDGRAPH;

 END;
RUN;
```

Figure 13-1. *The nested structure of a graph template*

LAYOUT statements include the following styles:

- LAYOUT GRIDDED and LAYOUT DATAPANEL: Allow you to create a grid of graph cells with the same dimensions and properties (see Figure 13-2)

- LAYOUT LATTICE and LAYOUT DATALATTICE: Allow you to create a grid of graph cells with different dimensions and properties (see Figure 13-3)

- LAYOUT OVERLAY (or LAYOUT PROTOTYPE inside LAYOUT DATALATTICE and LAYOUT DATAPANEL): Lets you to create a single graph cell with one or more overlaid plots (see Figure 13-4)

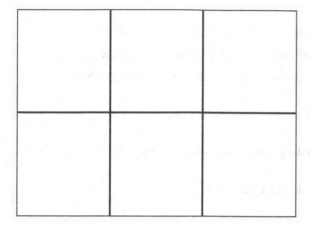

Figure 13-2. *The arrangement of cells in LAYOUT GRIDDED and LAYOUT DATAPANEL*

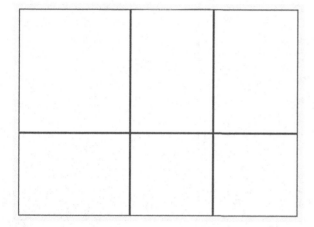

Figure 13-3. *The arrangement of cells in LAYOUT LATTICE and LAYOUT DATALATTICE*

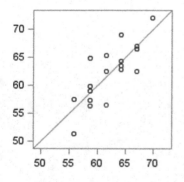

Figure 13-4. *A cell in LAYOUT OVERLAY and LAYOUT PROTOTYPE*

PLOT statements include the following:

- SERIESPLOT: Allows you to create a plot of connected points (see Figure 13-5)

- SCATTERPLOT: Lets you create a plot of symbols at specified points (see Figure 13-6)

- NEEDLEPLOT: Allows you to create a plot of vertical lines joining the horizontal zero axis line to each point (see Figure 13-7)

- REFERENCELINE: Lets you draw a line on the graph parallel with the x-axis or y-axis (see Figure 13-8)

- LINEPARM: Allows you to draw a line on the graph with a specified starting position and slope (see Figure 13-9)

- DISCRETELEGEND: Lets you create a legend (see Figure 13-10)

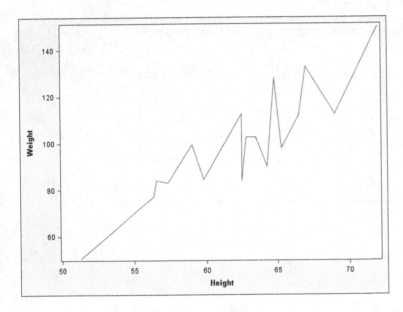

Figure 13-5. A SERIESPLOT example

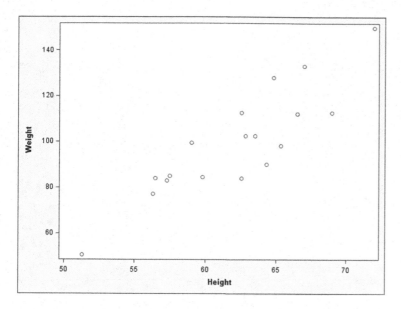

Figure 13-6. *A SCATTERPLOT example*

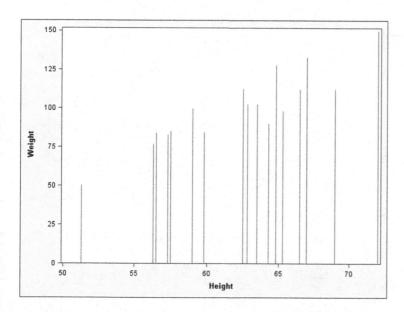

Figure 13-7. *A NEEDLEPLOT example*

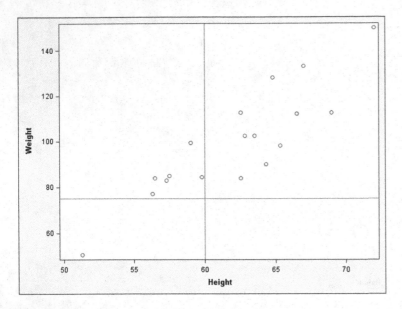

Figure 13-8. *A vertical and horizontal REFERENCELINE example*

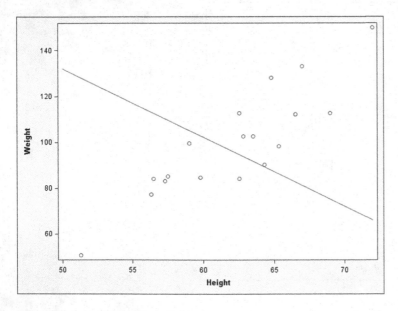

Figure 13-9. *A LINEPARM example*

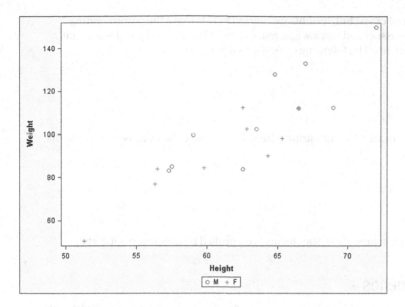

Figure 13-10. *A DISCRETELEGEND example*

Template Syntax

The following sections provide details of specific template syntax that is used later in this chapter.

What Does DYNAMIC Do?

If you are familiar with SAS macro programming, then you will notice that the DYNAMIC statement in a template provides functionality similar to the list of parameters in parentheses supplied to a macro. For example

```
DYNAMIC _var1 _var2 _var3;
```

This is referenced in PROC SGRENDER as follows:

```
DYNAMIC _var1 = "age" _var2 = "height" _var3 = "sex";
```

The only major difference between macro parameters and DYNAMIC variables is that it is not possible to set default values for DYNAMIC variables.

Specifying Titles and Footnotes

Title and footnote parameters are necessary for flexible templates. The generated template includes a single ENTRYTITLE statement. For example:

```
ENTRYTITLE 'This is a title';
ENTRYFOOTNOTE 'This is a footnote';
```

This may not be sufficient in all cases; but, fortunately, any ENTRYTITLE and the corresponding ENTRYFOOTNOTE statement with no associated text are ignored, so a template can include the maximum reasonable number of both statements. The following code shows two titles:

```
ENTRYTITLE 'Title A';
ENTRYTITLE;
ENTRYTITLE 'Title C';
```

You can insert a blank title by using an empty string. The following code shows three titles, with the second title blank:

```
ENTRYTITLE 'Title A';
ENTRYTITLE ' ';
ENTRYTITLE 'Title C';
```

The default formatting of the text from these statements is controlled by the current ODS style.

Specifying Axes and Legends

Unlike in traditional SAS/GRAPH, you don't usually need to specify axes when plotting with ODS Graphics, because the default settings based on the data are fairly good. However, when the graphics include more than one graph panel with a common axis, you may need to remove one of the axes and keep the sizes of the graph panels consistent.

The LAYOUT statement has options that only show the common axes on the outside edge:

```
LAYOUT LATTICE / ROWDATARANGE = UNION;
                /* common row axes */
LAYOUT LATTICE / COLUMNDATARANGE = UNION;
                /* common column axes */
```

The same is true for secondary axes:

```
LAYOUT LATTICE / ROW2DATARANGE = UNION;
                /* common secondary row axes */
LAYOUT LATTICE / COLUMN2DATARANGE = UNION;
                /* common secondary column axes */
```

COLUMNAXES and ROWAXES

COLUMNAXES and ROWAXES have the same function of replacing column and row axes, respectively, in existing layouts. They act like additional LAYOUT statements to hold COLUMNAXIS or ROWAXIS statements that specify the properties of the common axis to be displayed. Note that if there are multiple columns of panels, you can specify a separate COLUMNAXIS statement for each column.

For example, the following code displays the x-axis below a single column of panels with all the axis ticks, tick values, and labels shown:

```
COLUMNAXES;
  COLUMNAXIS / DISPLAY = (LABEL LINE TICKS TICKVALUES);
ENDCOLUMNAXES;
```

You can find an examples of COLUMNAXES in the section "Enhancing a Template: Adding Labels to Points."

SIDEBAR

It is possible to specify SIDEBAR areas around the graph area using the ALIGN= option, which has four possible values: TOP, LEFT, RIGHT, and BOTTOM. These areas are located outside the axis areas. By default, the contents are stretched to fill the entire width of the area, so using SPACEFILL=FALSE is recommended. A common use of these areas is to move DISCRETELEGEND statements from the LAYOUT OVERLAY area to below all the panels. Here's an example:

```
SIDEBAR / ALIGN = BOTTOM SPACEFILL = FALSE;
  DISCRETELEGEND "scatter" / TITLE = _grouplabel ORDER = ROWMAJOR
                 BORDER = TRUE BORDERATTRS = (COLOR = BLACK);
ENDSIDEBAR;
```

This code generates the legend shown in Figure 13-11.

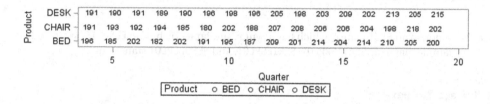

Figure 13-11. A SIDEBAR legend with SPACEFILL=FALSE

If you use SPACEFILL=TRUE, which is the default setting, the generated legend changes to the one shown in Figure 13-12.

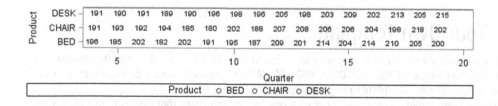

Figure 13-12. A SIDEBAR legend with SPACEFILL=TRUE

You can find another example of SIDEBAR in the section "Enhancing a Template: Adding Labels to Points."

IF

You can use the IF statement to conditionally include a single template statement that can be used in this template and that is followed by an ENDIF statement. The IF clause can include most Data step functions, such as EXISTS() which checks whether a variable exists. Note that the IF clause is never followed by a semi-colon and utilizes standard SAS WHERE statement expressions:

```
IF (EXISTS(age) AND EXISTS(weight))
  SCATTERPLOT X = age Y = weight;
ENDIF;
```

IF can also be used to conditionally include multiple statements, like SCATTERPLOT and SERIESPLOT statements, where the first statement is effectively included in the IF construct. Both SCATTERPLOT and SERIESPLOT are included within the IF ... ENDIF clause:

```
IF (EXISTS(age) AND EXISTS(weight))
  SCATTERPLOT X = age Y = weight;
  SERIESPLOT X = age Y = weight;
ENDIF;
```

There is also the option of an ELSE clause, which has a syntax similar to IF, but no ELSE IF is currently available. Here is an example that uses SCATTERPLOT, SERIESPLOT, and NEEDLEPLOT statements:

```
IF (EXISTS(_scatter))
  SCATTERPLOT X = age Y = weight;
  SERIESPLOT X = age Y = weight;
ELSE
  NEEDLEPLOT X = age Y = weight;
ENDIF;
```

You can find more examples of IF clauses in the sections "Adding Conditional Features: Handling Missing Arguments" and "Adding Conditional Features: Optional Reference Lines."

Creating Your Own Templates

Graph templates are not easy to simplify, so it is recommended that you use a graph template generator (such as ODS Graphics Designer, PROC SGPLOT, or PROC SGSCATTER) to create a basic graph template. You can then manually improve the template to fit your requirements.

It is important to remember when developing your own graph templates that they can only be applied to a single SAS data set, so planning the input data set can be almost as important as designing the template. Therefore, if the graph template requires data from several different input data sets, these data sets must be combined into a single data set before rendering. Note that missing values should not affect the graph's appearance, provided the data is sorted appropriately.

Graph templates let you overlay many different plots within the same axes. This makes the templates easier to generalize with parameters rather than with hard-coded values.

Customizing PROC SGSCATTER Graphs

PROC SGSCATTER graphs can be limited in their basic forms, so it's useful to be able to take a simple graph and enhance it to create a more relevant graph. The following sections explain how to add new cell to a basic PROC SGSCATTER graph.

Generating a Simple Template with PROC SGSCATTER

PROC SGSCATTER is an ideal starting point to develop multipanel graphs where the individual plots are similar but not identical. You can use the PLOT statement to plot a series of different combinations of variables from the same data set as scatter plots in separate panels. The following example demonstrates the basic code:

```
PROC SGSCATTER DATA = sashelp.class
               TMPLOUT = 'sgscatter.sas';
  TITLE 'Class details';
  PLOT (height weight) * age height * weight / GROUP = sex;
RUN;
```

Note that this code produces three scatter plots: height*age, weight*age, and height*weight. By default, PROC SGSCATTER arranges plots in a 2 × 2 grid, so the three plots should appear in three of the four cells. The GROUP= option is equivalent to the y*x=group syntax from PROC GPLOT, but it's applied to every plot.

The generated template code (from SAS 9.3; only the DESIGNWIDTH= and DESIGNHEIGHT= options are missing in SAS 9.2), stored in sgscatter.sas, is as follows:

```
proc template;
  define statgraph sgscatter;
    begingraph / designwidth=640 designheight=640;
      EntryTitle "Class details" /;
      layout gridded;
        layout lattice / pad=(top=5) rowgutter=10
                columngutter=10 columns=2;
          ScatterPlot X=Age Y=Height /
                      primary=true Group=Sex NAME="PLOT";
          ScatterPlot X=Age Y=Weight / primary=true Group=Sex;
          ScatterPlot X=Weight Y=Height /
                      primary=true Group=Sex;
        endlayout;
        DiscreteLegend "PLOT" / order=rowmajor title="Sex";
      endlayout;
    endgraph;
  end;
run;
```

The graph, generated with the SAS-supplied ODS Journal style, which has been designed for publications, is shown in Figure 13-13.

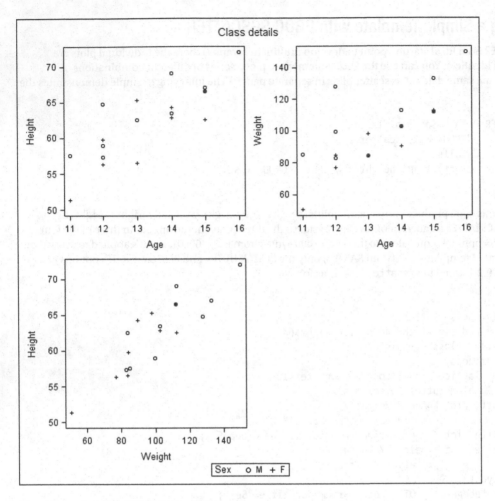

Figure 13-13. PROC SGSCATTER graph

Adding DYNAMIC Parameters to the Template

After being reformatted to match the other SAS code in this chapter, the generated template is as follows. Hard-coded items to be converted to parameters are bolded and the template names are underlined:

```
PROC TEMPLATE;
  DEFINE STATGRAPH sgscatter;
    BEGINGRAPH / DESIGNWIDTH = 640 DESIGNHEIGHT = 640;
      ENTRYTITLE "Class details" /;
      LAYOUT GRIDDED;
        LAYOUT LATTICE /
                PAD = (TOP = 5) ROWGUTTER = 10
                COLUMNGUTTER = 10 COLUMNS=2;
          SCATTERPLOT X = Age Y = Height /
                      PRIMARY = TRUE GROUP = Sex NAME = "plot";
          SCATTERPLOT X = Age Y = Weight /
```

```
                        PRIMARY = TRUE GROUP = Sex;
            SCATTERPLOT X = Weight Y = Height /
                        PRIMARY = TRUE GROUP = Sex;
        ENDLAYOUT;
        DISCRETELEGEND "plot" / ORDER = ROWMAJOR TITLE = "Sex";
      ENDLAYOUT;
    ENDGRAPH;
  END;
RUN;
```

The aim of adding parameters to a template is to allow it to be used with data sets other than the data set used during its development. The data set variables Age, Height, Weight, and Sex can be replaced with _var1, _var2, _var3, and _group. The legend title Sex can also be converted to the parameter grouplabel. All these new parameters are specified on the DYNAMIC statement:

```
PROC TEMPLATE;
  DEFINE STATGRAPH sgscatter;
    DYNAMIC _var1 _var2 _var3 _group _grouplabel;
    BEGINGRAPH / DESIGNWIDTH = 640 DESIGNHEIGHT = 640;
      ENTRYTITLE "Class details" /;
      LAYOUT GRIDDED;
        LAYOUT LATTICE /
                PAD = (TOP = 5) ROWGUTTER = 10
                COLUMNGUTTER = 10 COLUMNS = 2;
          SCATTERPLOT X = _var1 Y = _var2 /
                      PRIMARY = TRUE GROUP = _group
                      NAME = "plot";
          SCATTERPLOT X = _var1 Y = _var3 /
                      PRIMARY = TRUE GROUP = _group;
          SCATTERPLOT X = _var3 Y = _var2 /
                      PRIMARY = TRUE GROUP = _group;
        ENDLAYOUT;
        DISCRETELEGEND "plot" / ORDER = ROWMAJOR
                      TITLE = _grouplabel;
      ENDLAYOUT;
    ENDGRAPH;
  END;
RUN;
```

Title and footnote parameters are a necessity for flexible templates. The updated template includes three ENTRYTITLE and three ENTRYFOOTNOTE statements, with parameters for each one.

This template is being updated to increase its flexibility, so you're encouraged to remove any hard-coded values. That means DESIGNWIDTH= and DESIGNHEIGHT= should be removed from the BEGINGRAPH statement.

217

Replacing the Template Name

Finally, ODS Graphics Designer and each of the procedures give their generated templates a name. The procedures use specific names that, without alteration, would restrict the number of templates available for use. It is therefore strongly recommended that you change the default template name—in this case, sgscatter—to something a little more descriptive (such as scatter_2x2):

```
PROC TEMPLATE;
  DEFINE STATGRAPH scatter_2x2;
    DYNAMIC _var1 _var2 _var3 _group _grouplabel
            _title1 _title2 _title3
            _footnote1 _footnote2 _footnote3;
    BEGINGRAPH /;
      ENTRYTITLE _title1 /;
      ENTRYTITLE _title2 /;
      ENTRYTITLE _title3 /;
      LAYOUT GRIDDED;
        LAYOUT LATTICE /
                PAD = (TOP = 5) ROWGUTTER = 10
                COLUMNGUTTER = 10 COLUMNS = 2;
          SCATTERPLOT X = _var1 Y = _var2 /
                      PRIMARY = TRUE GROUP = _group
                      NAME = "plot";
          SCATTERPLOT X = _var1 Y = _var3 /
                      PRIMARY = TRUE GROUP = _group;
          SCATTERPLOT X = _var3 Y = _var2 /
                      PRIMARY = TRUE GROUP = _group;
        ENDLAYOUT;
        DISCRETELEGEND "plot" / ORDER = ROWMAJOR
                      TITLE = _grouplabel;
      ENDLAYOUT;
      ENTRYFOOTNOTE _footnote1 /;
      ENTRYFOOTNOTE _footnote2 /;
      ENTRYFOOTNOTE _footnote3 /;
    ENDGRAPH;
  END;
RUN;
```

Having converted the generated template to use parameters, it is a good idea to test it to make sure it creates the intended graph from sashelp.class:

```
PROC SGRENDER DATA = sashelp.class
            TEMPLATE = 'scatter_2x2';
  DYNAMIC _var1 = 'Age' _var2 = 'Height' _var3 = 'Weight'
          _group = 'Sex' _grouplabel = 'Sex'
          _title1 = 'Class details';
RUN;
```

The template has been generalized and made more useful, and it is now ready to be used with another SAS data set (for example, sashelp.cars):

```
PROC SGRENDER DATA = sashelp.cars
              TEMPLATE = 'scatter_2x2';
  DYNAMIC _var1 = 'EngineSize' _var2 = 'Horsepower'
          _var3 = 'MPG_City'
          _group = 'Type' _grouplabel = 'Type'
          _title1 = 'Car comparison';
RUN;
```

The graph generated with the ODS Journal style is shown in Figure 13-14. Note that the variable labels in sashelp.cars are automatically used as the individual plot axis labels.

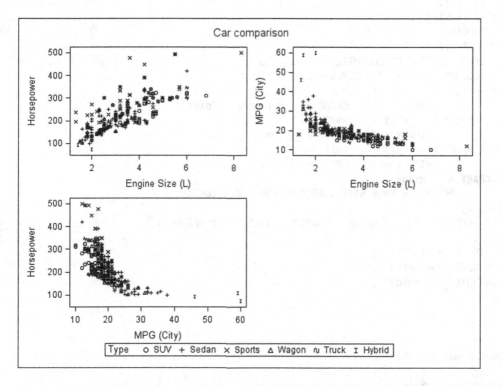

Figure 13-14. *A graph generated with the modified PROC SGSCATTER graph template using sashelp.cars*

Enhancing a Template: Adding a New Graph

This template currently has four panels and four variables, but only three plots. The legend only includes a list of values for the group variable, so a useful enhancement would be to include a bar chart of the group frequencies:

```
PROC TEMPLATE;
  DEFINE STATGRAPH scatter_2x2_bar;
    DYNAMIC _var1 _var2 _var3 _group _grouplabel
            _title1 _title2 _title3
            _footnote1 _footnote2 _footnote3;
    BEGINGRAPH /;
      ENTRYTITLE _title1 /;
      ENTRYTITLE _title2 /;
      ENTRYTITLE _title3 /;
      LAYOUT GRIDDED;
        LAYOUT LATTICE /
                PAD = (TOP = 5) ROWGUTTER = 10
                COLUMNGUTTER = 10 COLUMNS = 2;
          SCATTERPLOT X = _var1 Y = _var2 /
                      PRIMARY = TRUE GROUP = _group NAME = "plot";
          SCATTERPLOT X = _var1 Y = _var3 /
                      PRIMARY = TRUE GROUP = _group;
          SCATTERPLOT X = _var3 Y = _var2 /
                      PRIMARY = TRUE GROUP = _group;
          BARCHART X = _group /
                      PRIMARY = TRUE STAT = FREQ ORIENT = HORIZONTAL;
        ENDLAYOUT;
        DISCRETELEGEND "plot" / ORDER = ROWMAJOR TITLE = _grouplabel;
      ENDLAYOUT;
      ENTRYFOOTNOTE _footnote1 /;
      ENTRYFOOTNOTE _footnote2 /;
      ENTRYFOOTNOTE _footnote3 /;
    ENDGRAPH;
  END;
RUN;
```

The template is now ready for use:

```
PROC SGRENDER DATA = sashelp.cars
              TEMPLATE = 'scatter_2x2_bar';
  DYNAMIC _var1 = 'EngineSize' _var2 = 'Horsepower' _var3 = 'MPG_City'
          _group = 'Type' _grouplabel = 'Type'
          _title1 = 'Car comparison';
RUN;
```

The graph generated with the ODS Journal style is shown in Figure 13-15.

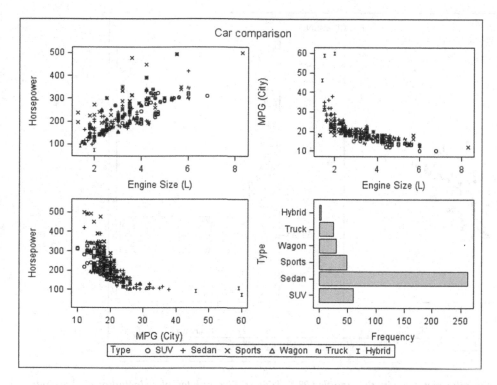

Figure 13-15. *A graph generated with the modified PROC SGSCATTER graph template including an extra bar chart using* sashelp.cars

Adding Conditional Features: Handling Missing Arguments

As it stands, this template is designed to plot information from four variables in four plots, three scatter plots, and one bar chart. However, all three variables may not always be used in the scatter plots; how does this template cope with just two scatter-plot variables?

```
PROC SGRENDER DATA = sashelp.cars
              TEMPLATE = 'scatter_2x2_bar';
  DYNAMIC _var1 = 'EngineSize' _var2 = 'Horsepower'
          _group = 'Type' _grouplabel = 'Type'
          _title1 = 'Car comparison';
RUN;
```

Unfortunately, this code gives the following log warnings:

```
WARNING: The SCATTERPLOT statement will not be drawn because one or more
 of the required arguments were not supplied.
WARNING: The SCATTERPLOT statement will not be drawn because one or more
 of the required arguments were not supplied.
```

221

But the graph is still created, as shown in Figure 13-16.

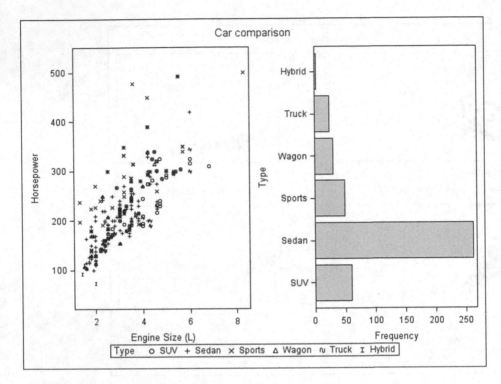

Figure 13-16. *A graph generated with the modified PROC SGSCATTER graph template including an extra bar chart using sashelp.cars, but with only two cells populated*

Omitting the _group= and _grouplabel= values as shown here

```
PROC SGRENDER DATA = sashelp.cars
            TEMPLATE = 'scatter_2x2_bar';
  DYNAMIC _var1 = 'EngineSize' _var2 = 'Horsepower' _var3 = 'MPG_City'
          _title1 = 'Car comparison';
RUN;
```

which produces the following log warning:

WARNING: The BARCHART statement will not be drawn because one or more of the required arguments were not supplied.

However, the graph in Figure 13-17 is created, with the unexpected legend label.

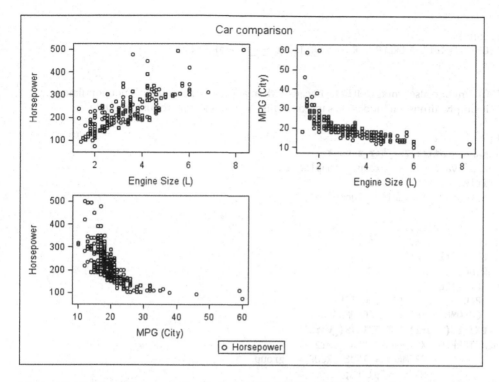

Figure 13-17. *A graph generated with the modified* PROC SGSCATTER *graph template using* sashelp.cars *with the group= and grouplabel= values omitted*

You can prevent these log warnings and unexpected legend labels by using conditional processing statements in the template. The IF statement can be used to conditionally include a single template statement, which can be used in this template. However, IF cannot be used to conditionally include multiple statements, like LAYOUT clauses, so its usefulness may be limited.

To prevent the warning messages, you can include the PLOT statements only when all the required variables are present. Note that the IF clause is never followed by a semicolon and uses standard SAS WHERE statement expressions:

```
IF (EXISTS(_var1) AND EXISTS(_var2))
    SCATTERPLOT X = _var1 Y = _var2 /
            PRIMARY = TRUE GROUP = _group NAME = "plot";
ENDIF;
IF (EXISTS(_var1) AND EXISTS(_var3))
    SCATTERPLOT X = _var1 Y = _var3 /
            PRIMARY = TRUE GROUP = _group;
ENDIF;
IF (EXISTS(_var3) AND EXISTS(_var2))
    SCATTERPLOT X = _var3 Y = _var2 /
            PRIMARY = TRUE GROUP = _group;
ENDIF;
IF (EXISTS(_group))
    BARCHART X = _group /
            PRIMARY = TRUE STAT = FREQ ORIENT = HORIZONTAL;
```

```
ENDIF;
IF (EXISTS(_group))
    DISCRETELEGEND "plot" / ORDER = ROWMAJOR TITLE = _grouplabel;
ENDIF;
```

The EXISTS() function also works well here, because when a DYNAMIC parameter is not populated by PROC SGRENDER, it simply "drops out" and ceases to exist. This produces a more robust template:

```
PROC TEMPLATE;
  DEFINE STATGRAPH scatter_2x2_bar_robust;
    DYNAMIC _var1 _var2 _var3 _group _grouplabel
            _title1 _title2 _title3
            _footnote1 _footnote2 _footnote3;
    BEGINGRAPH /;
      ENTRYTITLE _title1 /;
      ENTRYTITLE _title2 /;
      ENTRYTITLE _title3 /;
      LAYOUT GRIDDED;
        LAYOUT LATTICE /
                PAD = (TOP = 5) ROWGUTTER = 10
                COLUMNGUTTER = 10 COLUMNS = 2;
          IF (EXISTS(_var1) AND EXISTS(_var2))
            SCATTERPLOT X = _var1 Y = _var2 /
                        PRIMARY = TRUE GROUP = _group
                        NAME = "plot";
          ENDIF;
          IF (EXISTS(_var1) AND EXISTS(_var3))
            SCATTERPLOT X = _var1 Y = _var3 /
                        PRIMARY = TRUE GROUP = _group;
          ENDIF;
          IF (EXISTS(_var3) AND EXISTS(_var2))
            SCATTERPLOT X=_var3 Y=_var2 /
                        PRIMARY = TRUE GROUP = _group;
          ENDIF;
          IF (EXISTS(_group))
            BARCHART X = _group /
                     PRIMARY = TRUE STAT = FREQ
                     ORIENT = HORIZONTAL;
          ENDIF;
        ENDLAYOUT;
        IF (EXISTS(_group))
          DISCRETELEGEND "plot" /
                          ORDER = ROWMAJOR TITLE = _grouplabel;
        ENDIF;
      ENDLAYOUT;
      ENTRYFOOTNOTE _footnote1 /;
      ENTRYFOOTNOTE _footnote2 /;
      ENTRYFOOTNOTE _footnote3 /;
    ENDGRAPH;
  END;
RUN;
```

The following PROC SGRENDER code uses the robust template:

```
PROC SGRENDER DATA = sashelp.cars
               TEMPLATE = 'scatter_2x2_bar_robust';
  DYNAMIC _var1 = 'EngineSize' _var2 = 'Horsepower' _var3 = 'MPG_City'
          _title1 = 'Car comparison';
RUN;
```

Now the graph shown in Figure 13-18 is created, without the unnecessary legend and without any log warnings.

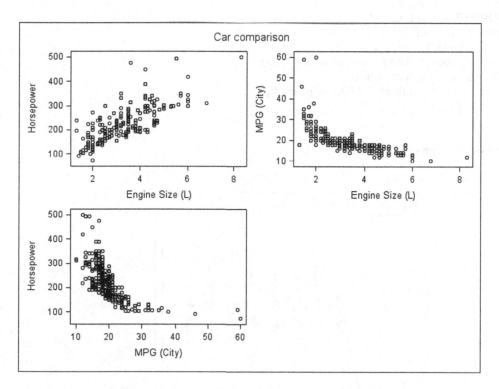

Figure 13-18. *A graph generated with the modified PROC SGSCATTER graph template using sashelp.cars, with robust error checking*

The previous PROC SGRENDER code with the full set of parameters still produces the full graph, as before.

Customizing PROC SGPLOT Templates

PROC SGPLOT can produce a wide range of single-cell graphs. But adding an additional cell to contain a legend requires template code, as explained next.

Generating a Simple Template with PROC SGPLOT

PROC SGPLOT is intended to produce single plots. Both PROC SGPANEL and PROC SGSCATTER can produce single plots, but that is not what they are designed to do, and the options available in these procedures are more limited. All three procedures use the current ODS style to supply information regarding color, fonts, sizes, and patterns to display in the plot being generated. This may not be exactly what is required, so customizations can override these defaults.

The following code uses the plotdata_ods data set created earlier to generate one or more overlaid lines with error bars at each point and a horizontal reference line:

```
PROC SGPLOT DATA = plotdata_ods
            TMPLOUT = 'sgplot.sas';
  TITLE 'Standard Error of Sales';
  SCATTER X = visitnum Y = value1 /
          GROUP = product YERRORLOWER = value1_lower
          YERRORUPPER = value1_upper;
  SERIES X = visitnum Y = value1 / GROUP = product;
  REFLINE 1100 / AXIS = Y;
RUN;
```

This produces the graph shown in Figure 13-19.

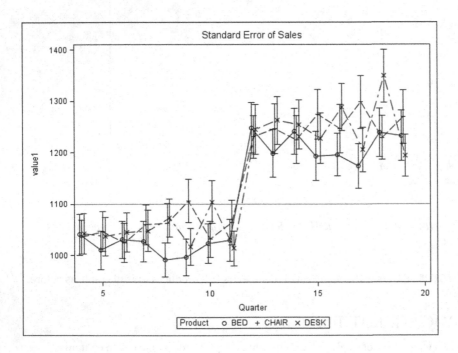

Figure 13-19. *A PROC SGPLOT graph*

The following template is also generated. It will be used as the starting point for customization:

```
proc template;
  define statgraph sgplot;
    begingraph /;
      EntryTitle "Standard Error of Sales" /;
      layout overlay;
        ScatterPlot X=visitnum Y=value1 /
          primary=true Group=PRODUCT
          YErrorUpper=value1_upper YErrorLower=value1_lower
          LegendLabel="value1" NAME="SCATTER";
        SeriesPlot X=visitnum Y=value1 /
          Group=PRODUCT LegendLabel="value1"
          NAME="SERIES";
        ReferenceLine y=1100 / clip=true;
        DiscreteLegend "SCATTER"/ title="Product";
      endlayout;
    endgraph;
  end;
run;
```

Adding DYNAMIC Parameters to the Template

After being reformatted to match the other SAS code in this chapter, the generated template is as follows. Hard-coded items to be converted to parameters are bolded:

```
PROC TEMPLATE;
  DEFINE STATGRAPH sgplot;
    BEGINGRAPH /;
      ENTRYTITLE "Standard Error of Sales" /;
      LAYOUT OVERLAY;
        SCATTERPLOT X = visitnum Y = value1 /
                    PRIMARY = TRUE GROUP = product
                    YERRORUPPER = value1_upper
                    YERRORLOWER = value1_lower
                    LEGENDLABEL = "value1" NAME = "scatter";
        SERIESPLOT X = visitnum Y = value1 /
                    GROUP = product LEGENDLABEL = "value1"
                    NAME = "series";
        REFERENCELINE Y = 1100 / CLIP = TRUE;
        DISCRETELEGEND "scatter"/ TITLE = "Product";
      ENDLAYOUT;
    ENDGRAPH;
  END;
RUN;
```

The aim of adding parameters to a template is to allow its use with data sets other than the one used during its development. The data-set variables Visitnum, Value1, Value1_lower, Value1_upper, and Product can be replaced with _xvar, _yvar1, _yvar1_lower, _yvar1_upper, and _group. The legend title Product can also be converted to the parameter _grouplabel, and the reference-line value can be converted to _yintercepta. All these new parameters are specified in the DYNAMIC statement:

```
PROC TEMPLATE;
  DEFINE STATGRAPH sgplot;
    DYNAMIC _xvar _yvar1 _yvar1_lower _yvar1_upper
            _group _grouplabel
            _yintercepta;
    BEGINGRAPH /;
      ENTRYTITLE "Standard Error of Sales" /;
      LAYOUT OVERLAY;
        SCATTERPLOT X = _xvar Y = _yvar1 /
                    PRIMARY = TRUE GROUP = _group
                    YERRORUPPER = _yvar1_upper
                    YERRORLOWER = _yvar1_lower
                    NAME = "scatter";
        SERIESPLOT X = _xvar Y = _yvar1 /
                    GROUP = _group NAME="series";
        REFERENCELINE Y = _yintercepta / CLIP = TRUE;
        DISCRETELEGEND "scatter" / TITLE = _grouplabel;
      ENDLAYOUT;
    ENDGRAPH;
  END;
RUN;
```

In the same way that the template from PROC SGSCATTER had ENTRYTITLE and ENTRYFOOTNOTE statements added, this template needs a similar number of titles and footnotes available to users. It is also reasonable to make this new template unique by updating the template name (for example, sgplot_dynamic):

```
PROC TEMPLATE;
  DEFINE STATGRAPH sgplot_dynamic;
    DYNAMIC _xvar _yvar1 _yvar1_lower _yvar1_upper
            _group _grouplabel
            _yintercepta
            _title1 _title2 _title3
            _footnote1 _footnote2 _footnote3;
    BEGINGRAPH /;
      ENTRYTITLE _title1 /;
      ENTRYTITLE _title2 /;
      ENTRYTITLE _title3 /;
      LAYOUT OVERLAY;
        SCATTERPLOT X = _xvar Y = _yvar1 /
                    PRIMARY = TRUE GROUP = _group
                    YERRORUPPER = _yvar1_upper
                    YERRORLOWER = _yvar1_lower
                    NAME = "scatter";
```

```
         SERIESPLOT X = _xvar Y = _yvar1 /
                      GROUP = _group NAME = "series";
         REFERENCELINE Y = _yintercepta / CLIP = TRUE;
         DISCRETELEGEND "scatter" / TITLE = _grouplabel;
       ENDLAYOUT;
       ENTRYFOOTNOTE _footnote1 /;
       ENTRYFOOTNOTE _footnote2 /;
       ENTRYFOOTNOTE _footnote3 /;
     ENDGRAPH;
   END;
RUN;
```

Having converted the generated template to use parameters, it is a good idea to test it to make sure it creates the intended graph from `plotdata_ods`:

```
PROC SGRENDER DATA = plotdata_ods
              TEMPLATE = 'sgplot_dynamic';
  DYNAMIC _xvar = 'Visitnum' _yvar1 = 'Value1'
          _yvar1_lower = 'Value1_lower'
          _yvar1_upper = 'Value1_upper'
          _group = 'Product' _grouplabel = 'Product'
          _yintercepta = 1100
          _title1 = 'Standard Error of Sales';
RUN;
```

Enhancing a Template: Adding Labels to Points

There is currently no information about how many data values contribute to each point on the graph. However, a variable in `plotdata_ods` (`ccount`) contains this information in character format, so a useful enhancement would be to include these values somewhere.

You can draw a separate graph panel with a common x-axis scale below the main graph, so the values are aligned with the points on the graph, and plot text values as data points in a row per group. The `MARKERCHARACTER=` and `MARKERCHARACTERATTRS=` options of the `SCATTERPLOT` statement make this very easy to achieve. The `LAYOUT LATTICE` statement determines the relative height of each panel in the lattice, and the `_nvar1` parameter provides the value to be plotted in the new panel.

Finally, in order to position the legend below the new panel, you move the `DISCRETELEGEND` statement into a `SIDEBAR` located at the bottom of the graph, using the `SPACEFILL=FALSE` option so the legend is not stretched across the entire width of the `SIDEBAR`:

```
PROC TEMPLATE;
  DEFINE STATGRAPH sgplot_marker;
    DYNAMIC _xvar _yvar1 _yvar1_lower _yvar1_upper
            _group _grouplabel
            _yintercepta
            _nvar1
            _title1 _title2 _title3
            _footnote1 _footnote2 _footnote3;
    BEGINGRAPH /;
      ENTRYTITLE _title1 /;
      ENTRYTITLE _title2 /;
```

```
      ENTRYTITLE _title3 /;
      LAYOUT LATTICE /
             COLUMNS = 1 ROWS = 2 COLUMNDATARANGE = UNION
             ROWWEIGHTS = (0.85 0.15);
        LAYOUT OVERLAY;
          SCATTERPLOT X = _xvar Y = _yvar1 /
                      PRIMARY = TRUE GROUP = _group
                      YERRORUPPER = _yvar1_upper
                      YERRORLOWER = _yvar1_lower
                      NAME = "scatter";
          SERIESPLOT X = _xvar Y = _yvar1 /
                      GROUP = _group NAME = "series";
          REFERENCELINE Y = _yintercepta / CLIP = TRUE;
        ENDLAYOUT;
        LAYOUT OVERLAY;
          SCATTERPLOT X = _xvar Y = _group /
                      PRIMARY = TRUE GROUP = _group
                      MARKERCHARACTERATTRS = (COLOR = BLACK)
                      MARKERCHARACTER = _nvar1;
        ENDLAYOUT;
        COLUMNAXES;
          COLUMNAXIS / DISPLAY = (LABEL LINE TICKS TICKVALUES);
        ENDCOLUMNAXES;
        SIDEBAR / ALIGN = BOTTOM SPACEFILL = FALSE;
          DISCRETELEGEND "scatter" / TITLE = _grouplabel
          ORDER = ROWMAJOR;
        ENDSIDEBAR;
      ENDLAYOUT;
      ENTRYFOOTNOTE _footnote1 /;
      ENTRYFOOTNOTE _footnote2 /;
      ENTRYFOOTNOTE _footnote3 /;
    ENDGRAPH;
  END;
RUN;
```

The template is now ready for use:

```
PROC SGRENDER DATA = plotdata_ods
              TEMPLATE = 'sgplot_marker';
  DYNAMIC _xvar = 'Visitnum' _yvar1 = 'Value1'
          _yvar1_lower = 'Value1_lower'
          _yvar1_upper = 'Value1_upper'
          _group = 'Product' _grouplabel = 'Product'
          _yintercepta = 1100
          _nvar1 = 'ccount'
          _title1 = 'Standard Error of Sales';
RUN;
```

This code string generates the graph shown in Figure 13-20.

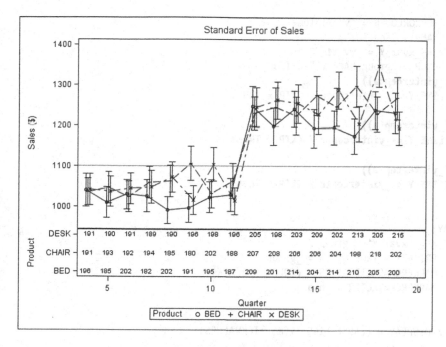

Figure 13-20. *A graph generated with the PROC SGPLOT graph template including an embedded legend*

Adding Conditional Features: Optional Reference Lines

As it stands, this template will always generate a single reference line. But you may need two, three, or even no reference lines. You can use the IF statement to provide this flexibility by adding two more reference line parameters, _yinterceptb and _yinterceptc, and making all the reference lines dependent on values being specified. This produces a more robust template:

```
PROC TEMPLATE;
  DEFINE STATGRAPH sgplot_count;
    DYNAMIC _xvar _yvar1 _yvar1_lower _yvar1_upper
            _group _grouplabel
            _yintercepta _yinterceptb _yinterceptc
            _nvar1
            _title1 _title2 _title3
            _footnote1 _footnote2 _footnote3;
    BEGINGRAPH /;
      ENTRYTITLE _title1 /;
      ENTRYTITLE _title2 /;
      ENTRYTITLE _title3 /;
      LAYOUT LATTICE /
             COLUMNS = 1 ROWS = 2 COLUMNDATARANGE = UNION
             ROWWEIGHTS = (0.85 0.15);
        LAYOUT OVERLAY;
          SCATTERPLOT X = _xvar Y = _yvar1 /
                      PRIMARY = TRUE GROUP = _group
                      YERRORUPPER = _yvar1_upper
```

```
                        YERRORLOWER = _yvar1_lower
                        NAME = "scatter";
        SERIESPLOT X = _xvar Y = _yvar1 /
                        GROUP = _group NAME = "series";
        IF (EXISTS(_yintercepta))
          REFERENCELINE Y = _yintercepta / CLIP = TRUE;
        ENDIF;
        IF (EXISTS(_yintercepta))
          REFERENCELINE Y = _yinterceptb / CLIP = TRUE;
        ENDIF;
        IF (EXISTS(_yintercepta))
          REFERENCELINE Y = _yinterceptc / CLIP = TRUE;
        ENDIF;
      ENDLAYOUT;
      LAYOUT OVERLAY;
        SCATTERPLOT X = _xvar Y = _group /
                        PRIMARY = TRUE GROUP = _group
                        MARKERCHARACTERATTRS = (COLOR = BLACK)
                        MARKERCHARACTER = _nvar1;
      ENDLAYOUT;
      COLUMNAXES;
        COLUMNAXIS / DISPLAY = (LABEL LINE TICKS TICKVALUES);
      ENDCOLUMNAXES;
      SIDEBAR / ALIGN = BOTTOM SPACEFILL = FALSE;
        DISCRETELEGEND "scatter" / TITLE = _grouplabel
                        ORDER = ROWMAJOR;
      ENDSIDEBAR;
    ENDLAYOUT;
    ENTRYFOOTNOTE _footnote1 /;
    ENTRYFOOTNOTE _footnote2 /;
    ENTRYFOOTNOTE _footnote3 /;
  ENDGRAPH;
 END;
RUN;
```

The previous PROC SGRENDER code, with the same set of parameters, still produces the same graph.

Graph Template Contents

The following templates were generated by the ODS Graphics Designer earlier in this book.

Template A

Note that in SAS 9.2 there is no CLUSTERWIDTH= parameter, and the generated code does not include the PROC SGRENDER step:

```
proc template;
define statgraph sgdesign;
dynamic _AGE;
begingraph;
```

```
  entrytitle halign=center 'Vertical bar title';
  entryfootnote halign=left 'Vertical bar footnote';
  layout lattice / rowdatarange=data columndatarange=data
                   rowgutter=10 columngutter=10;
    layout overlay;
      barchart x=_AGE / name='bar' stat=freq clusterwidth=1.0;
    endlayout;
  endlayout;
endgraph;
end;
run;
proc sgrender data=SASHELP.CLASS template=sgdesign;
dynamic _AGE="AGE";
run;
```

Template B

Comparing this new generated template with the original graph Template A, you see that multiple panels are achieved using LAYOUT DATALATTICE around LAYOUT PROTOTYPE, instead of LAYOUT LATTICE around LAYOUT OVERLAY:

```
proc template;
define statgraph sgdesign;
dynamic _AGE _SEX;
dynamic _panelnumber_;
begingraph;
  entrytitle halign=center 'Vertical bar title';
  entryfootnote halign=left 'Vertical bar footnote';
  layout datalattice columnvar=_SEX / cellwidthmin=1 cellheightmin=1
                     rowgutter=3 columngutter=3 rowdatarange=unionall
                     row2datarange=unionall columndatarange=unionall
                     column2datarange=unionall
                     headerlabeldisplay=value;
    layout prototype;
      barchart x=_AGE / name='bar' stat=freq barwidth=0.85
               clusterwidth=0.85;
    endlayout;
  endlayout;
endgraph;
end;
run;
proc sgrender data=SASHELP.CLASS template=sgdesign;
dynamic _AGE="AGE" _SEX="SEX";
run;
```

Template C

Comparing this new generated template with the original graph Template B, you see that multiple panels are achieved using LAYOUT DATAPANEL around LAYOUT PROTOTYPE, instead of LAYOUT LATTICE around LAYOUT OVERLAY:

```
proc template;
define statgraph sgdesign;
dynamic _AGE _SEX2;
dynamic _panelnumber_;
begingraph;
  entrytitle halign=center 'Vertical bar title';
  entryfootnote halign=left 'Vertical bar footnote';
  layout datapanel classvars=(_SEX2) / cellwidthmin=1 rowgutter=3
                   columngutter=3 rowdatarange=unionall
                   row2datarange=unionall columndatarange=unionall
                   column2datarange=unionall headerlabeldisplay=value
                   rows=1 columns=2;
    layout prototype / ;
      barchart x=_AGE / name='bar' stat=freq barwidth=0.85
               clusterwidth=0.85;
    endlayout;
  endlayout;
endgraph;
end;
run;
proc sgrender data=SASHELP.CLASS template=sgdesign;
dynamic _AGE="AGE" _SEX2="SEX";
run;
```

Template D

The generated template includes a LAYOUT LATTICE around two LAYOUT OVERLAY sections. Note that the GROUPDISPLAY= and CLUSTERWIDTH= parameters and the PROC SGRENDER step are not available in SAS 9.2:

```
proc template;
define statgraph Graph;
dynamic _AGE _AGE2 _HEIGHT;
begingraph;
  entrytitle halign=center 'Panel title';
  entryfootnote halign=left 'Panel footnote';
  layout lattice / rowdatarange=data columndatarange=data rows=2
                   rowgutter=10 columngutter=10;
    layout overlay;
      barchart x=_AGE / name='bar' stat=freq groupdisplay=Cluster
               clusterwidth=1.0;
    endlayout;
    layout overlay;
      scatterplot x=_AGE2 y=_HEIGHT / name='scatter';
    endlayout;
```

```
  endlayout;
endgraph;
end;
run;
proc sgrender data=SASHELP.CLASS template=Graph;
dynamic _AGE="AGE" _AGE2="AGE" _HEIGHT="HEIGHT";
run;
```

Conclusions

You can use manual updates to generated graph templates to create useful customized templates. By using incremental updates, you can assess the impact of each change.

■ ■ ■

## CHAPTER 14

ODS GRAPHICS Statement

When using the SG procedures—PROC SGPLOT, PROC SGPANEL, PROC SGSCATTER, and PROC SGRENDER—the ODS GRAPHICS statement is optional. However, doing so can change a number of important features of the output image (such as the size and file format); and with new SAS versions, ODS Graphics supports new image formats. In particular, this chapter examines the EMF image-file format in more detail, because it changes significantly across SAS versions.

In the same way that you can use ODS to prepare output suitable for other applications, you can use the ODS GRAPHICS statement to create graphs in specific formats depending on your need. This chapter explains them all.

ODS GRAPHICS Statement

The ODS GRAPHICS statement is used to switch the output of ODS Graphics on and off, but you can also use it to specify the default features of any graphs produced. The basic syntax is as follows:

```
ODS GRAPHICS {ON} {/ option(s)};
ODS GRAPHICS OFF;
```

Options include those shown in Table 14-1.

Table 14-1. ODS GRAPHICS Options

Option	Usage
IMAGEFMT Specifies the output format used to generate image or vector graphic files. For example, IMAGEFMT=PNG. This option has been replaced by OUTPUTFMT from SAS 9.3.	The default is STATIC. Version-specific information is provided in the next section.
IMAGEFILE Specifies the base image filename. For example: IMAGEFILE="C:\temp\image".	The default name is the output object, the default folder is the current folder, and the suffix is set by IMAGEFMT.
HEIGHT Specifies the height of any graph. For example: HEIGHT=8cm.	The default is the value of the SAS registry entry ODS > STATISTICAL GRAPHICS > Design Height, or the value of the DESIGNHEIGHT= option in a STATGRAPH template.
WIDTH Specifies the width of any graph. For example: WIDTH=10cm.	The default is the value of the SAS registry entry ODS > STATISTICAL GRAPHICS > Design Width, or the value of the DESIGNWIDTH= option in a STATGRAPH template.

ODS Graphics Output Destinations

ODS Graphics output destinations included in SAS 9.2, SAS 9.3, and SAS 9.4.

SAS 9.2

The ODS GRAPHICS ON statement is not required before any of the SG procedures—PROC SGPLOT, PROC SGPANEL, PROC SGSCATTER, and PROC SGRENDER—but it is required if the DATA step is used to render data with graph templates or if you want to generate ODS graphics from other SAS procedures. The output destinations are listed in Table 14-2.

Table 14-2. *Output Destinations in SAS 9.2*

Output Destination	Supported Image File Types: IMAGEFMT=
HTML	PNG (default), GIF, JPEG, JPG
LISTING	PNG (default), BMP, DIB, EMF, EPSI, GIF, JFIF, JPEG, JPG, PBM, PDF, PS, SASEMF, STATIC, TIFF, WMF
LATEX	PS (default), EPSI, GIF, PNG, PDF, JPG
PDF, PCL (PRINTER), and PS (PRINTER)	PNG (default), JPEG, JPG, GIF
RTF	PNG (default), JPEG, JPG, JFIF
Markup tagsets	All markup family tagsets have the default value built in.

SAS 9.3

The ODS GRAPHICS ON statement is no longer required in the interactive environments of SAS 9.3 (including Enterprise Guide) on Windows, Unix, and Linux platforms, because it is automatically switched on by default whenever you start an interactive SAS session. All batch SAS sessions, as well as interactive SAS sessions on other platforms, behave the same way as in SAS 9.2, unless the SAS options relating to the default behavior have been changed.

The documentation only mentions the OUTPUTFMT= option for specifying the output image file format, but IMAGEFMT= still works as an alternative, so there is no need to change your existing programs yet. The output destinations are listed in Table 14-3.

Table 14-3. *Output Destinations in SAS 9.3*

Output Destination	Supported Image File Types: OUTPUTFMT=
HTML	PNG (default), GIF, JPEG, JPG, PBM, SVG, EMF, BMP
LISTING	PNG (default), BMP, DIB, EMF, EPSI, GIF, JFIF, JPEG, JPG, PBM, PDF, PS, SASEMF, STATIC, TIFF, WMF, XBM, XPM, PSL, SVG
LATEX	PS (default), EPSI, GIF, PNG, PDF, JPG, PSL, EPS, EMF
PDF and PCL (PRINTER)	SVG (default), JPEG, JPG, GIF, PSL, EPS, EPSI, PDF, PCL, PNG, EMF
PS (PRINTER)	PNG (default), JPEG, JPG, GIF, PSL, EPS, EPSI, PDF, PCL, EMF
RTF	PNG (default), JPEG, JPG, JFIF, EMF
Markup tagsets	All markup family tagsets have the default value built in.

SAS 9.4

The documentation only mentions the OUTPUTFMT= option for specifying the output image file format, but IMAGEFMT= still works as an alternative, so there is no need to change your existing programs yet. The output destinations are listed in Table 14-4.

Table 14-4. *Output Destinations in SAS 9.4*

Output Destination	Supported Image File Types: OUTPUTFMT=
EPUB	PNG (default), GIF, JPG, SVG
HTML	PNG (default), GIF, JPEG, JPG, PBM, SVG, EMF, BMP
HTML5	SVG (default), PNG, GIF, JPEG, JPG, PBM, EMF, BMP
LISTING	PNG (default), BMP, DIB, EMF, EPSI, GIF, JFIF, JPEG, JPG, PBM, PDF, PS, SASEMF, STATIC, TIFF, WMF, XBM, XPM, PSL, SVG
PDF and PCL (PRINTER)	SVG (default), JPEG, JPG, GIF, PSL, EPS, EPSI, PDF, PCL, PNG, EMF
POWERPOINT	PNG (default), JPEG, JPG, GIF, EPS, EMF, BMP, CGM, TIFF
PS (PRINTER)	PNG (default), JPEG, JPG, GIF, PSL, EPS, EPSI, PDF, PCL, EMF
RTF	EMF (default), PNG, JPEG, JPG, JFIF
Markup tagsets	All markup family tagsets have the default value built in.

EMF Output Files

EMF output file formats included in SAS 9.2, SAS 9.3, and SAS 9.4 are available for use in the ODS RTF destination, but not in ODS HTML or ODS PDF destination.

SAS 9.2

EMF files are supposed to be vector files that can be increased in size without impacting the plot detail. But in SAS 9.2 they are actually rendered files, rather than vector files, so zooming into the plots will eventually result in pixelation:

```
ODS GRAPHICS / IMAGEFMT = EMF;
```

or

```
ODS GRAPHICS / IMAGEF MT = SASEMF;
```

SAS 9.3

In SAS 9.3, EMF files are vector files and generate much better plots than SASEMF:

```
ODS GRAPHICS / OUTPUTFMT = EMF;
```

or

```
ODS GRAPHICS / OUTPUTFMT = SASEMF;
```

To display a full page of a report in an EMF file, there is an EMF printer device:

```
ODS PRINTER PRINTER = EMF;
```

There are, however, some limitations:

- Footnotes are limited to 132 characters.
- Plots should not be zoomed beyond their original dimensions. Therefore, it is recommended that you create EMF files with the maximum dimensions at which they are expected to be viewed.

SAS 9.4

Further improvements have been made to the EMF image formats in SAS 9.4:

```
ODS GRAPHICS / OUTPUTFMT = EMF;
```

or

```
ODS GRAPHICS / OUTPUTFMT = SASEMF;
```

To display a full page of a report in an EMF file, there are now three EMF printer devices:

```
ODS PRINTER PRINTER = EMF;
```

or

```
ODS PRINTER PRINTER = SASEMF;
```

or

```
ODS PRINTER PRINTER = EMFDUAL;
```

Conclusions

Software evolves over time and versions, so it is recommended that you periodically review your ODS GRAPHICS usage to make sure you're using the full extent of the current SAS version's features.

Index

Get the eBook for only $5!

Why limit yourself?

Now you can take the weightless companion with you wherever you go and access your content on your PC, phone, tablet, or reader.

Since you've purchased this print book, we're happy to offer you the eBook in all 3 formats for just $5.

Convenient and fully searchable, the PDF version enables you to easily find and copy code—or perform examples by quickly toggling between instructions and applications. The MOBI format is ideal for your Kindle, while the ePUB can be utilized on a variety of mobile devices.

To learn more, go to www.apress.com/companion or contact support@apress.com.

Printed in the United States
By Bookmasters